Shire County Guide 2

LINCOLNSHIRE

David Kaye

Shire Publications Ltd

Published in 1995 by Shire Publications Ltd, Cromwell House, Church Street, Princes Risborough, Buckinghamshire HP27 9AA, UK.
Copyright © 1995 by David Kaye. First published 1984; second edition 1989; third edition 1995. Shire County Guide 2. ISBN 0 7478 0271 8.

Printed in Great Britain by CIT Printing Services, Press Buildings, Merlins Bridge, Haverfordwest, Dyfed SA61 1XF.

British Library Cataloguing in Publication Data
Kaye, David
Lincolnshire. – 3Rev.ed. – (Shire County Guides; No. 2)
I. Title II. Series
914.25304859
ISBN 0-7478-0271-8

Acknowledgements

Photographs are acknowledged as follows: David Kaye, pages 11, 18, 20, 21, 24, 36, 37, 45, 49, 54, 57, 61, 62, 65, 70 (bottom), 71, 72, 73 (both), 76, 83, 88 (top), 91, 95, 101, 105, 108, 113, 119; Kingston upon Hull City Council, Public Relations Department, page 110; Cadbury Lamb, cover and pages 14, 15, 16, 17, 22, 23, 25, 27 (both), 28, 29, 33 (both), 35, 41, 47, 48 (top), 51, 52, 55, 56, 60, 67, 69, 70 (top), 75 (both), 77, 78, 79, 81 (both), 82, 84 (both), 85, 86, 87, 89, 92, 93, 96 (both), 98, 99, 102, 104, 106, 107, 109, 115, 116, 118 (both), 120; Roger Taylor, pages 40 (both), 48 (bottom), 88 (bottom).
The map of Lincolnshire on pages 4-7 and the street plan of Lincoln on page 34 are by Robert Dizon.

Ordnance Survey grid references

Although information on how to reach most of the places described in this book by car is given in the text, National Grid References are also included in many instances, particularly for the harder-to-find places in chapters 3, 4, 5 and 9, for the benefit of those readers who have the Ordnance Survey 1:50,000 Landranger maps of the area. The references are stated as a Landranger sheet number followed by the 100 km National Grid square and the six-figure reference.

To locate a site by means of the grid references, proceed as in the following example: St Ives Cross, Sutton St James (OS 131: TF 388182). Take the OS Landranger map sheet 131 ('Boston and Spalding area'). The grid numbers are printed in blue around the edges of the map. In more recently produced maps these numbers are repeated at 10 km intervals throughout the map, so that it is not necessary to open it out completely.) Read off these numbers from the left along the top edge of the map until you come to 38, denoting a vertical grid line, then estimate eight-tenths of the distance to vertical line 39 and envisage an imaginary vertical grid line 38.8 at this point. Next look at the grid numbers at one side of the map (either side will do) and read *upwards* until you find the horizontal grid line 18. Estimate two-tenths of the distance to the next horizontal line above (i.e. 19), and so envisage an imaginary horizontal line across the map at 18.2. Follow this imaginary line across the map until it crosses the imaginary vertical line 38.8. At the intersection of these two lines you will find St Ives Cross.

The Ordnance Survey Landranger maps which cover Lincolnshire are sheets 112, 113, 121, 122, 130 and 131. Very small areas of the county are found on maps 141, and 142.

Cover: *Boston 'Stump' and the river Witham.*

Contents

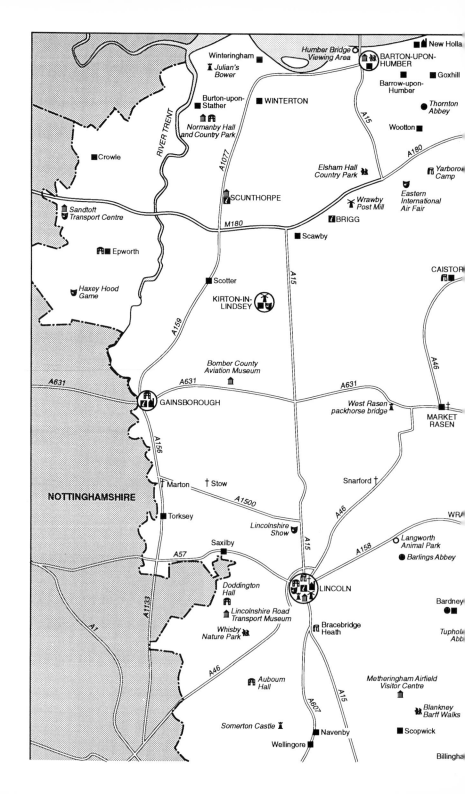

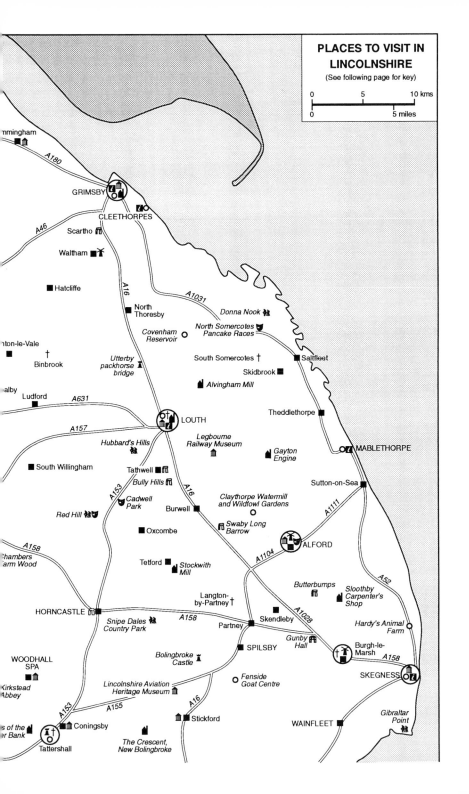

PLACES TO VISIT IN
LINCOLNSHIRE
(See following page for key)

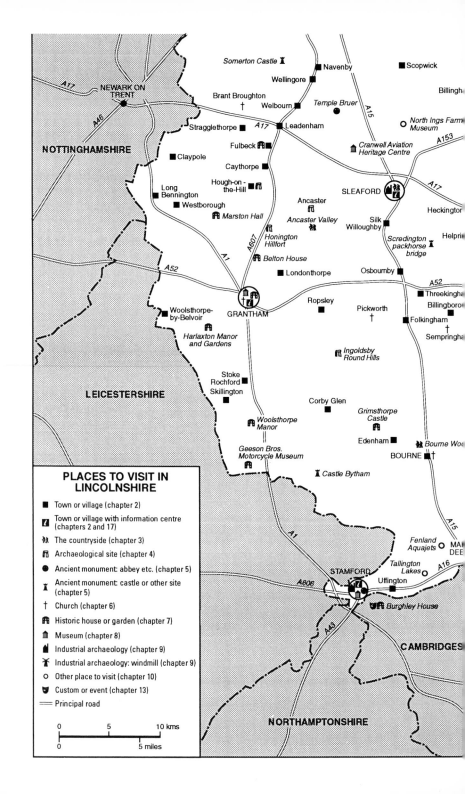

Somerton Castle ⚔   Navenby ■   ■ Scopwick

Wellingore ■

Billingh■

Brant Broughton
†   Welbourn ■   Temple Bruer ●

NEWARK ON
TRENT

A17   A46   A15

NOTTINGHAMSHIRE

Stragglethorpe ■   A17   Leadenham ■

○ North Ings Farm
Museum

A153

Fulbeck 🏰■   🏛 Cranwell Aviation
Heritage Centre

A17

■ Claypole

Caythorpe ■

SLEAFORD 🏰ℹ

Heckingtor

Long   Hough-on-   ■🏰
Bennington ■   the-Hill

Ancaster
🏰

■ Westborough

Ancaster Valley 🐾   Silk
Willoughby   Helpri■

🏰 Marston Hall

Screcington ⚔
packhorse
bridge

A607   A1   Honington
Hillfort

🏰 Belton House

■ Londonthorpe   Osbournby ■

A52   A52

GRANTHAM 🏛ℹ   Ropsley
■   Pickworth
†   ■ Threekingh■

Billingboro■

Woolsthorpe-
by-Belvoir ■
🏰   Folkingham ■

Sempringha■

Harlaxton Manor
and Gardens   🏛 Ingoldsby
Round Hills

Stoke
Rochford ■
Skillington   Corby Glen
■   Grimsthorpe
Castle
🏰

LEICESTERSHIRE

🏰 Woolsthorpe
Manor   Edenham ■   🐾 Bourne Woo

Geeson Bros.
Motorcycle Museum
🏭   BOURNE ■†

⚔ Castle Bytham

PLACES TO VISIT IN
LINCOLNSHIRE

■ Town or village (chapter 2)

ℹ Town or village with information centre
(chapters 2 and 17)

🐾 The countryside (chapter 3)

🏰 Archaeological site (chapter 4)

● Ancient monument: abbey etc. (chapter 5)

⚔ Ancient monument: castle or other site
(chapter 5)

† Church (chapter 6)

🏰 Historic house or garden (chapter 7)

🏛 Museum (chapter 8)

▮ Industrial archaeology (chapter 9)

🕇 Industrial archaeology: windmill (chapter 9)

○ Other place to visit (chapter 10)

♥ Custom or event (chapter 13)

═══ Principal road

Fenland
Aquajets ○   ○ MA■
DEE

A1   A15

Tallington
Lakes ○   A16

STAMFORD ℹ   Uffington ○

A606   🏛🏰 Burghley House

A43   CAMBRIDGES

0   5   10 kms

0   5 miles

NORTHAMPTONSHIRE

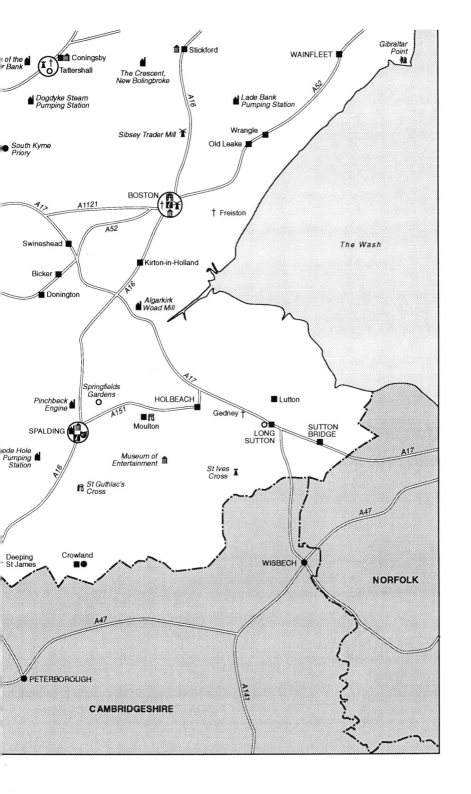

of the
Bank

🔔✝ Coningsby
Tattershall

🏛 Stickford

WAINFLEET

Gibraltar
Point

The Crescent,
New Bolingbroke

Dogdyke Steam
Pumping Station

Lade Bank
Pumping Station

A52

Sibsey Trader Mill

Wrangle

South Kyme
Priory

Old Leake

A16

BOSTON

✝ Freiston

The Wash

A17   A1121

A52

Swineshead

Kirton-in-Holland

Bicker

A16

Donington

Algarkirk
Woad Mill

A17

Springfields
Gardens

HOLBEACH

Lutton

Pinchbeck
Engine

A151

Gedney ✝

SUTTON
BRIDGE

SPALDING

Moulton

LONG
SUTTON

A17

ode Hole
Pumping
Station

Museum of
Entertainment

St Ives
Cross

A16

St Guthlac's
Cross

A47

Deeping
St James

Crowland

WISBECH

NORFOLK

A47

A47

PETERBOROUGH

A141

CAMBRIDGESHIRE

Preface

Welcome to the Shire County Guide to Lincolnshire, one of over thirty such books, written and designed to enable you to organise your time in the county well.

The Shire County Guides fill the need for a compact, accurate and thorough guide to each county so that visitors can plan a half-day excursion or a whole week's stay to best advantage. Residents, too, will find the guides a handy and reliable reference to the places of interest in their area.

Travelling British roads can be time consuming, and the County Guides will ensure that you need not inadvertently miss any interesting feature in a locality, that you do not accidentally bypass a new museum or an outstanding church, that you can find an attractive place to picnic, and that you will appreciate the history and the buildings of the towns or villages in which you stop.

This book has been arranged in special interest chapters, such as the countryside, historic houses and gardens or archaeological sites, and all these places of interest are located on the map on pages 4-7. Use the map either for an overview to decide which area has most to interest you, or to help you enjoy your immediate neighbourhood. Then refer to the nearest town or village in chapter 2 to see, at a glance, what special features or attractions each community contains or is near. The subsequent chapters enable readers with a particular interest to find immediately those places of importance to them, while the cross-referencing under 'Towns and villages' assists readers with wider tastes to select how best to spend their time.

1
The parts of Lincolnshire

Until April 1974 the area covered in this book, the historic county of Lincolnshire, was divided into three separate counties, based on the historic 'Parts' of Lincolnshire, known as Holland, Kesteven and Lindsey, with their county towns respectively at Boston, Sleaford and Lincoln. With the local government reorganisation of that year Parts of Holland and Kesteven and the southern portion of Parts of Lindsey were formed into the new county of Lincolnshire, with Lincoln as its county town, whilst the remainder of Lindsey was incorporated, along with large areas of Yorkshire, into the new county of Humberside, with its headquarters at Beverley. As this third edition goes to press, further reorganisation is planned and it is likely that Humberside County Council will be abolished and its functions south of the Humber taken over by unitary local authorities combining the roles of the former district and county councils.

Those who do not know this region imagine that Lincolnshire is as flat as the Fens, but large tracts are as high as hills in most other English counties. Indeed at Normanby-le-Wold (near Caistor) the Wolds reach a height of 550 feet (168 metres).

The Wolds

The Lincolnshire Wolds are a southern continuation of the Yorkshire Wolds, which cross North Humberside, reaching the Humber estuary to the west of Hull. They stretch for over 40 miles (64 km) in a south-easterly direction, with the Kirmington Gap near their northern end. Less than 5 miles (8 km) wide at the northern end, they spread out to almost 15 miles (24 km) in the south. These are chalk hills where this material tapers in the south to only 2 miles (3 km) wide, the rest being Spilsby sandstone, especially around Horncastle, where many churches are built of this greenstone. Chalk is also used for churches, Legbourne for example. There is an outcrop of red chalk at Red Hill, Goulceby.

A few rivers have their sources in the Wolds, such as the Bain, the Lud and the Rase, but many valleys have become dry combes since post-glacial times. Man used the tops of the Wolds as trackways and as burial sites (see chapter 4).

Only a few fragments of downland grass remain of the thousands of acres that supported huge sheep populations, especially in the fifteenth and sixteenth centuries, bringing prosperity to market towns like Louth, but causing the depopulation of many small villages. In the twentieth century grain crops have replaced the pastures, and in recent years an ever expanding crop of oilseed rape turns these hillsides bright yellow each May. Perhaps the best main road to drive along to appreciate the full majesty of the Wolds is the A153 from Horncastle to Louth.

Lincoln Cliff

Lincoln Cliff, also known as Lincoln Edge, and as Lincoln Heath to the south of the city of Lincoln, is a limestone ridge that stretches from Winteringham on the Humber in the north to Stamford, on the southern border of Lincolnshire, a distance of about 70 miles (110 km). It is, however, very narrow until it reaches the Grantham area, where it widens into the traditional heartlands of Kesteven (a Celtic name meaning woodlands). It is pierced by the river Witham in a narrow valley at Lincoln, whilst there is a higher, dry pass further south called the Ancaster Gap. It contains the sources of the rivers Ancholme, Brant, Glen and Slea.

Iron ore has been worked in the area to the north of Scunthorpe and in the Grantham region, whilst the ridge has also provided excellent building stone at Ancaster and over the border at Barnack (Cambridgeshire), Clipsham and Ketton (Leicestershire). This geographical feature is named the Lincoln

Cliff or Edge because although its eastern slope up from the Fens and the valleys of the Ancholme and Witham is gentle it is steep in places on its western slope, sometimes dropping as two steps (as along the A17 on either side of Leadenham). For the best scenic tour of this ridge the A607 between Lincoln and Grantham is recommended.

The Wolds and Lincoln Cliff proved in both world wars to be ideal places for the construction and operation of military airfields, although only Barkston Heath, Cranwell, Scampton and Waddington still remain active. As with the Wolds, cereal crops are the main agricultural use of the Edge today.

The Fens

Most of the Lincolnshire Fenland is made up of silt. The southern part, consisting of the former Parts of Holland and the eastern section of Parts of Kesteven, were drained with varying degrees of success, from medieval times onwards, but the more northerly wetlands in Parts of Lindsey, such as East Fen, West Fen and Wildmore Fen, were not properly drained until the first half of the nineteenth century, with the construction of catchwater drains and the introduction of steam pumping engines. The Romans used the Fens for stock rearing and constructed roads and a canal in the area. In medieval times cattle were raised here, as well as sheep, the profits from which enabled the building of such magnificent churches as those at Fleet and Gedney, near Holbeach. The large tracts of monastic lands, especially those owned by Crowland Abbey, aided the prosperity of this part of the county. The monks were also responsible for the construction and maintenance of causeways across the Fens, like the one between Threekingham and Donington (the present A52), with its small monastic house at Bridge End.

With the great agricultural depression towards the close of the nineteenth century the Fenland farmers had to find new crops. Eventually the three products that most people associate with Lincolnshire – potatoes, tulips and sugar beet – became established. Although sugar beet was established earlier in Norfolk, it was not until the passing of the British Sugar (Subsidy) Act in 1925 that the Lincolnshire industry started in earnest. Soon three factories were built and prospering at Bardney, Brigg and Spalding, as well as others just outside the county at King's Lynn, Peterborough and Newark. The growing of tulips has become nationally famous through the annual Tulip Parade. Potatoes, after harvesting, are stored in long mounds called 'graves' or 'pies'. The best main roads to give an impression of the Fens are the A16 and the A17.

Lindsey Marshes

Between the Wolds and the North Sea lies a band of marshland, about 10 miles (16 km) in width, but it was once more extensive, much land having been lost through coastal erosion between Grimsby and Skegness. Farming here has suffered serious setbacks when the sea has broken through the natural sand dunes. In 1287, 1288, 1335, 1571, 1801 and 1953 there were such disasters.

In 1953 20,000 acres (8000 hectares) were flooded and forty-three people lost their lives. As a consequence of these inundations settlements have usually been built on slight rises, and this is best illustrated by the deserted village site of Stain, near Withern and just off the A157 (TF 468847).

Saltmaking by the evaporation of sea water was an important industry on these marshes from the iron age onwards, as well as in the Fens. The Domesday Book mentions salt pans at such villages along the present A1031 coastal road as Tetney, Marsh Chapel and Grainthorpe. One of the principal routes for this trade was probably the present B1200 through Saltfleetby. In more recent times the stocky, short Lincoln Red cattle have been bred in this area, although now much of the land is down to cereal crops and oilseed rape.

The Humber Bank

Although much of what has been written about the Lindsey Marshes applies equally to the low-lying land on the south bank of the Humber, since the late eighteenth century man has found uses other than agriculture for this area. Extensive brick-earth deposits were dug into and bricks manufactured in the Barton-upon-Humber area. Brick from this source may well have been used as early as the late fourteenth century for the construction of Thornton Abbey. Since the early 1950s the petrochemical industry has moved into the part of the bank between Grimsby and Killingholme, and there are two oil refineries and two works producing titanium dioxide.

Grimsby has a very long history as a port, and from about 1850 until about 1975 was one of the world's leading fishing ports. In the twentieth century it became an important centre of the processed food industry, its products ranging from fish fingers to tinned peas, and from biscuits to fish meal. The town and the newer port of Immingham (opened in 1912) have close links with Scandinavia, in particular Norway.

Isle of Axholme

The name Axholme means 'the island of Haxey', still one of the principal settlements there and scene of the annual Hood Game (see page 120). Originally it was very fenny, with the villages and small towns sited on the higher ground along the spine of the 'island', the inhabitants of which are known as Isolonians. It is bounded on the north by the rivers Don and Ouse, on the east by the river Trent and on the south by the river Idle. To its west lies the boggy area known as Hatfield Chase, stretching towards Doncaster. After much local opposition it was drained by Cornelius Vermuyden and his Dutch team of engineers in the reign of Charles I.

At the time when the Reverend Samuel Wesley was Rector of Epworth (1696-1735) the main crop was flax, because of the area's dampness. However, today it is dry enough for the cultivation of wheat and even carrots. On its western extremity is the village of Wroot, the centre of rhubarb cultivation.

Towns and industry

Although Lincolnshire is usually thought of as an agricultural county, it also contains four of the principal engineering towns in the East Midlands. At Lincoln many new engineering achievements were pioneered, including the military tank and the steam excavator or shovel. Thousands of steam engines, including traction engines, steam wagons, steam rollers and fairground engines, bearing the famous names of Clayton & Shuttleworth, Ruston, Foster and Robey, were built there.

Two Inter City electric trains on the Leeds to Kings Cross service at Grantham station.

In the First World War fighter planes for the Royal Flying Corps were made in the city.

In Grantham, at the great Spitalgate Works of Richard Hornsby, the first commercial heavy oil (diesel) engine was built. Since 1933 Grantham has been the home of Aveling Barford, famous for their road rollers and huge dumper trucks.

At Gainsborough William Marshall established his Britannia Works, also renowned for tractors (including the Field Marshalls) and road rollers. These firms have supplied the world with agricultural machinery and many other high-quality engineering products.

Scunthorpe, from the firing of its first furnace in 1864, has become one of the great steel-producing towns in Britain, of which few others remain.

High-speed trains have brought Grantham within 64 minutes travelling time from King's Cross, and thus within range of London commuters. The opening of the Humber Bridge in 1981 has also brought Barton-upon-Humber and Brigg within road commuting distance of Hull.

The largest towns in Lincolnshire and South Humberside, with their populations, are Grimsby (92,596), Lincoln (76,660), Scunthorpe (66,609), Cleethorpes (35,507), Grantham (30,084) and Boston (26,397).

Since the passing of the Bank Holiday Act of 1871 one of the growing industries has been the holiday trade, and this was boosted by the opening of railway branch lines to Cleethorpes (1863), Skegness (1873), Mablethorpe (1877) and Sutton-on-Sea (1886). Although the last two seaside resorts have lost their railway, this has been more than compensated for by the increase in road traffic. In 1936 Sir Billy Butlin opened his holiday camp at Skegness, and at about the same time the first of thousands of caravans arrived on the coastal strip between Cleethorpes and Skegness. The equally profitable conference industry has become established following the opening of the Embassy Centre in Skegness in 1983.

'Yellowbellies'

Lincolnshire-born people are known as 'Yellowbellies'. The origins of this term are disputed, and suggested derivations have included a species of Fenland frog, the eels found in Fenland dykes (ditches), the poppy juices taken by inhabitants suffering from malaria, the dyed stomachs of sheep feeding from a mustard crop in the fields, and farm workers stripped to the waist and working with their backs to the sun – hence a brown back and a yellow belly. However, the most usual explanation is that the ornamental fastenings (or frogs) down the uniforms of the Lincolnshire Regiment were yellow.

That regiment (now part of the Second Battalion, Royal Anglian Regiment) has as its regimental march 'The Lincolnshire Poacher', which has become the folksong anthem of the county.

After the setting up of the new Lincolnshire County Council in 1974 it adopted Lincoln green (a pale shade) as one of its colours (the other being white) and the Lincoln Imp as its emblem.

2
Towns and villages

Aby
Claythorpe Watermill and Wildfowl
Gardens, page 109.

Alford
*Early closing Thursday; market day
Tuesday.*
Alford lies at the eastern foot of the Wolds and
at the western side of the Inner Marsh. Through
it run the A1104 Mablethorpe and A1111
Sutton-on-Sea roads, which are busy during
the holiday season. Along West Street traffic
passes the attractive thatched Manor House,
which is reputed to have been built in 1661. It
was restored by the Alford Civic Trust, which
runs a museum in part of the building.

Off West Street lies the Market Place,
where a general market is held each Tuesday
and a flourishing and expanding craft market
on Fridays during the summer.

Further along West Street is the parish
church of St Wilfrid, built of green sandstone
and restored in 1865-81 to plans drawn up by
Sir George Gilbert Scott. Although much of it
is in the Decorated style, the tower is Perpendicular. There are examples of fourteenth-
century stained glass in the chancel and north
chapel windows. The chancel contains a fine
monument to Sir Robert and Lady Elizabeth
Christopher, who died in the reign of Charles
II. Beyond the church is the five-sailed windmill of 1837.

The Alford Festival is held every year in
August.

Alford Manor House Museum, page 94;
Mawthorpe Museum, page 94; **Alford
Tower Mill**, page 101; **Alford Festival**, page
122.

*In the locality: Claythorpe Watermill and
Wildfowl Gardens, page 109; Sloothby carpenter's shop, page 106.*

Algarkirk
Algarkirk Woad Mill, page 101.

Alkborough
'Julian's Bower' turf maze, page 68.

Alvingham
Alvingham Mill, page 101.

Aubourn
Aubourn Hall, page 82.

Bardney
Dominating Bardney is the British Sugar Corporation factory, which was opened in 1927.
Gone is the famous abbey where thousands of
pilgrims came to see St Oswald's remains.
Only earthworks survive. However, St Lawrence's church and its environs are well worth
a visit. Inside the 1434 church is the tomb slab
of Abbot Richard Horncastle (died 1508) and
some restored delightfully illustrated, charity
boards. Next to the church is Kitching's Free
School (founded 1711, rebuilt 1843) and the
Peter Hancock Hospital (1712) with an unusual memorial to Nine Squadron RAF.

Bardney Abbey, page 68.

*In the locality: Barlings Abbey, page 68;
Tupholme Abbey, page 73.*

Barrow-upon-Humber
Writing in 730, the Venerable Bede referred
to Barrow as 'Barauae'; he knew that by tradition the missionary to Mercia, St Chad, had
founded a monastery here. Of that early foundation nothing remains, but this former market town is well worth a visit, for at one time
it was also a port, from which sailed one of
the ferries that crossed the Humber to Hessle.

On Cross Hill is the remnant of a medieval
market cross.

Holy Trinity church contains a portrait of
John Harrison. The son of a Pontefract carpenter, he moved to Barrow when he was
four. Although himself apprenticed as a carpenter, his main interest was in clocks and
watches, for which he invented the gridiron

pendulum. In 1735 he won the Board of Longitude's £20,000 prize for an accurate sea chronometer that would also record a ship's longitude. However, he had to wait until 1773 to receive the money! In the churchyard outside is a sundial designed by his brother James.

Three-quarters of a mile (1200 metres) to the north on the banks of the Humber are the double motte and bailey earthworks called Barrow Castles, the date of which is uncertain.

In the locality: Thornton Abbey, page 72.

Barton-upon-Humber

Early closing Thursday; market day Monday.

Dominated by the Humber Bridge, which was opened on 24th June 1981 and has a central suspension span of 4626 feet (1410 metres), the longest in the world, this town is growing rapidly. In the time of the Domesday Book it was a more important port than Grimsby and it existed several centuries before Hull was established. It was the terminus of the Humber ferry to Hull before the railway began its route from New Holland in 1848.

The town is renowned for the Saxon tower of St Peter's church. However, St Peter's is really two churches in one: a small Anglo-Saxon structure (of which only two thirds still

stand) and a later thirteenth-century building. High up inside the west wall of the tower are two round windows, which originally had leather flaps instead of glass. Of the 70 foot (21 metre) tower, the topmost section may be post-Conquest. In the medieval church the east window of the north aisle is unique in that the mullion contains a crucifixion carving. The church was closed for worship in 1967 and is now in the care of English Heritage, which carried out extensive excavations in its interior in the early 1980s.

To the west stands St Mary's church, which was built at a time of changing architectural styles, as the nave pillars demonstrate. Those on the north side are heavy and dog-toothed, although not so rounded as true Norman ones, whilst those on the south side have eight slender shafts apiece. Yet probably less than a decade separates them. On the chancel floor is the brass of Simon Seman, a vintner (note the two wine barrels), who died in 1433.

Immediately to the east of St Peter's is Tyrwhitt Hall Barn, which has been restored. It may have been the medieval manorial hall.

Down on the banks of the Humber is an observation area for viewing the Humber Bridge. On the western side of the bridge lie Westfield Lakes, which became a nature reserve in 1983 and are on the site of the extensive clay pits. There are hides and the Peter

St Mary's church, Barton-upon-Humber.

Hodgkinson visitor centre.
Baysgarth Museum, page 94; **Humber Bridge Viewing Area**, page 110.

Belton
Belton House, page 82.

Bicker

In medieval times this village was a small port on an arm of the Wash. Now, since the land reclamation of the mid sixteenth century, it is 9 miles (14 km) from salt water! It lies on the busy holiday route to Skegness, the A52, beside which is the Old Red Lion inn, parts of which date from 1665. At the time of the Domesday survey Bicker had twenty-two salt pans and much of the village land was used for grazing cattle. Now it is rich arable land.

A quiet stroll through the village along the banks of the two streams that once flowed into Bicker Haven is well worth while. These are lined with trees and with comfortable houses in dark red brick. St Swithin's church has a fine but short Norman nave with a central tower (like other churches in the vicinity). There are some blocks of Anglo-Saxon interlaced carvings in the aisles and porch.

Billingborough

This large village on the B1177 is on the western edge of the Kesteven Fens. St Andrew's church spire reaches a height of 150 feet (46 metres) and is in the Decorated style. The nave appears to have been built in the fourteenth century, but the chancel dates only from 1891. The church is in a delightful setting, with Billingborough Hall to its north-west. This is said to have been built in 1620 but has some later additions. Of contemporary date is the George and Dragon inn. There is a pleasant pond down Church Lane. There are almost as many shops in Billingborough as in a small town.

In the locality: Sempringham church, page 80.

Billinghay

This large village lies on the banks of the canalised Billinghay Skirth, a tributary of the

St Andrew's church and the village pond at Billingborough.

nearby Witham. Pevsner describes it as 'close-knit and turning its back on the inhospitable Fen'. It is substantially built, with the modern Lafford Secondary School in contrast to the medieval church of St Michael, with its 1801 royal arms and commandments board.

Billinghay Cottage and Craft Workshop, page 109.

In the locality: Dogdyke Pumping Station, page 103; Tales of the River Bank, page 107.

Binbrook
Church of St Mary and St Gabriel, page 74.

Boothby Graffoe
Somerton Castle, page 69.

Boston

Early closing Thursday; market days Wednesday and Saturday.

The name of Boston comes from 'Botolph's Town', after the saint who is said to have founded a monastery near this site on the banks of the Witham in 654, although its

Market day in Boston, viewed from the top of the famous 'Stump'.

exact whereabouts have never been established. The town grew up originally as a suburb of the important village of Skirbeck, and the famous Boston 'Stump' was originally a mere chapel of ease. When it was rebuilt and enlarged at the beginning of the fourteenth century the huge tower was erected to a height of 272 feet (83 metres), the topmost section being in the form of an octagonal lantern to guide sailors coming up Boston Deeps and Haven. Visitors can at certain times climb to the base of this lantern. Unless visibility is excellent viewers may not be able to see as far as the Wash or Lincoln Cathedral as claimed in some guidebooks.

Boston obtained its charter from King John in 1204. The present docks were laid down in 1882 and there is a flourishing trade in importing timber and steel.

Famous Bostonians include John Foxe, the martyrologist and Puritan, who was born in the Market Place in 1516; the Reverend John Cotton, vicar of Boston, Lincolnshire, from 1612 to 1632 and of Boston, Massachusetts, from 1633 to 1652; the poetess Jean Ingelow (1820-97), famous for her poem 'High Tide

on the Coast of Lincolnshire, 1571' and for hymns; Herbert Ingram (1811-60) (see page 116), the founder of the *Illustrated London News* and member of Parliament for the town; and George Bass (who was born at Aswarby), the Royal Navy doctor and explorer after whom the Bass Strait is named (page 114).

The Guildhall in South Street was at one time the hall of the Guild of St Mary and dates from the fifteenth century. It contains the cells in which William Brewster, William Bradford and others of the Pilgrim Fathers were imprisoned in 1607, after their unsuccessful attempt to escape to Holland. Nearby are the elegant Custom House of 1725 and the Blackfriars' Hall in Spain Lane, which is 90 feet (27.5 metres) long and has been converted into a theatre and arts centre. A Georgian warehouse on the riverbank has also been renovated and put to use as the Sam Newsom Centre for music. Shodfriar's Hall looks an authentic Tudor timber-framed building but was rebuilt from its foundations in 1874.

On the eastern outskirts of the town is the Rochford Tower, built in red brick about 1510.

There is a similar structure in Skirbeck Road called the Hussey Tower.

Church of St Botolph, page 74; **Fydell House**, page 87; **Boston Guildhall**, page 94; **Maud Foster Mill**, page 102.

In the locality: Freiston church, page 75.

Bourne
Early closing Wednesday; market day Thursday.

Hereward the Wake is said to have been born in this town in about 1020. The extensive earthworks of his eleventh-century castle stand in the park to the south of the town centre. Bourne lies at the foot of the limestone hills of Kesteven and on the edge of the Fens, across which Bourne Eau flows to join the river Glen at Tongue End.

In the middle ages Bourne had the only house in Lincolnshire belonging to the small sub-order of Arrouasian canons; their church still stands. William Cecil (later first Baron Burghley) was born in the town centre in 1520.

Bourne was the home before the Second World War of the ERA racing cars and in the post-war period of the BRM motor-racing team under the direction of Raymond Mays, the racing driver, who was born here in 1899.

By the site of the former railway junction stands Red Hall, an early seventeenth-century house of dark red brick with ashlar quoins and a handsome Tuscan porch.

By the traffic lights in the centre of the town stands the Town Hall of 1821 with its Doric columns. Beyond the abbey church is the restored watermill, Baldock's Mill.

Bourne Abbey, page 74.

In the locality: Bourne Wood, page 61; Grimsthorpe Castle, page 90.

Brant Broughton
Church of St Helen, page 74; Friends' Meeting House, page 75.

Brigg
Early closing Wednesday; market day Thursday

Before 1872 Brigg did not exist as a separate entity but was divided between the parishes of Bigby, Broughton, Scawby and Wrawby. After that date it became the parish of Glanford Bridge (or Brigg).

The town owes its origins to two factors, the bridge over the river Ancholme and a famous fair. The fair was established by a royal charter from King John to Hugh Nevill in 1205, to be held annually about 5th August. Gypsies arrived there from all over England, galloping their horses for sale

The seventeenth-century Red Hall at Bourne.

The town hall at Brigg dates from 1817.

its grey brick exterior suggests, containing much gilding of lamp holders and door lintels.

The Dying Gladiator public house opposite in Bigby Street has a gory effigy above the entrance. Other attractive inns in the town centre are the Brocklesby Ox, named after a remarkable beast bred at Gedney in south Lincolnshire and painted by George Stubbs, and the White Hart.

In the locality: Elsham Hall Country and Wildlife Park, page 60; Wrawby Post Mill, page 108.

Burgh-le-Marsh

This former small market town on the A158 Skegness to Lincoln road used to be the terminus of a Roman road from Lincoln. Nearby, travellers transferred to a ferry for the journey across the Wash to the northern end of Peddars Way in Norfolk.

Cock Hill, the mound beside the main road just west of the church, is thought to have been a Saxon burial mound. Later it was heightened to form a cockpit, thus hiding the illegal activities from passers-by.

The Market Place is worth a visit with its Georgian and Victorian buildings. A useful town trail guide is available from the county library here, or from certain local shops.

The curfew bell is still rung at Burgh (pronounced as 'Borough') between Old Michaelmas Day and Old Lady Day (10th October until 5th April) at eight o'clock each evening. It is tolled long enough for anyone to repeat Psalm 130, followed by the tolling of the days of the month in tens.

The five-sailed windmill is still in working condition and dates from 1833. Keramikos Pottery is situated next to it in what used to be the miller's stables.

Church of St Peter and St Paul, page 75; **tower mill**, page 102.

In the locality: Gunby Hall, page 90.

Burton-upon-Stather

Situated on top of the cliff overlooking the lower reaches of the river Trent, this picturesque village has some charming cottages built out of clunch (a form of chalk). St Andrew's church is probably late twelfth-century and is in the Early English style.

around the streets, before bargains were sealed by a handslap. Percy Grainger recorded two separate versions of the traditional song about the fair, and his friend Frederick Delius used it as the basis for his tone poem *An English Rhapsody – Brigg Fair* in 1907.

St John the Evangelist's church dates from 1843 and is more attractive on the inside than

Among the monuments inside are an early fourteenth-century cross-legged knight (removed from Owston Ferry) and that of Sir Charles Sheffield (1776), whose family owned much land in this area and after whom the Sheffield Arms of 1830 (but founded in 1687) is named.

At the bottom of the steep village street there is a wharfside hamlet on the riverbank, where timber is imported.

Burwell

Although the name means 'the stream by the fort', neither are much in evidence, but the early eighteenth-century octagonal red brick butter cross is very prominent beside the busy A16 road south of Louth. Nowadays it is used as the village hall, but it is a reminder that originally Burwell had its own market in the latter half of the middle ages. Made redundant in 1981, St Michael's church is now maintained by the Redundant Churches Fund, partly because it contains a fragment of medieval wall painting near the chancel arch. Nearby stood the alien Benedictine priory, of which no vestige remains. The Stag's head inn is unusual for Lincolnshire in that its exterior (*c.*1900) is clad with hanging tiles, more reminiscent of East Sussex or Kent.

Caistor

Early closing Wednesday; market day Saturday.

Caistor was a small Roman town which covered 8 acres (3.2 hectares) and was given walls in the fourth century. Of these only a few inaccessible fragments remain, consisting mainly of rubble cores. Lying just below the western summit of the Wolds, this small town was connected to nearby High Street, a prehistoric ridgeway later used by the Romans to connect the Humber Bank with their other settlement in this area, Horncastle.

The parish church of Saints Peter and Paul has an Anglo-Saxon tower, to which sections in the Early English and Decorated styles were added during the middle ages. In the north aisle is an arched recess containing the tomb of Sir William de Hundon, a crusader. Also in this aisle, in a glass case, is the gad whip which until 1847 was cracked over the

vicar's head every Palm Sunday by a man from Broughton in payment for certain parcels of land.

The Market Square is well worth a visit, with its cast-iron Victoria Jubilee pump and handsome town houses, some dating from Georgian times, lining the west side.

North of the parish church is the picturesque Grammar School, parts of which date back to 1631 and are built of local ironstone. Nearby is the former Independent (Congregational) church of 1842, now the school's library, an imposing edifice with its Doric pillars.

The most famous figure of the past connected with the town is Sir Henry Newbolt (1862-1938), the poet of 'Drake's Drum', who was educated at the Grammar School.

Caythorpe

This is a large, yet compact village, with a wealth of mellow stone buildings, including Ivy House (1684) along High Street, which is a truly magnificent example of its period in this limestone area. The church has the comparatively rare dedication to St Vincent, although there are no less than eight such people of that name who have been canonised. Probably in this case it is meant to be St Vincent of Lerins, who lived on an island off the coast near Cannes in the fifth century and was described as a man 'pre-eminent in eloquence and learning'. Its entasis spire (looking rather like half a cucumber) reaches to a height of 156 feet (47 metres) and is similar in outline to that of Welbourn, also off the A607 Lincoln to Grantham road. It is one of only four churches in the whole of England to have a double nave, dating from the end of the thirteenth century, but restored by Sir George Gilbert Scott in 1860-1. Near the crest of the hill to the east of the village can be seen Caythorpe Court (1901-3), part of Lincolnshire College of Agriculture and Horticulture, constructed of Ancaster stone for Edgar Lubbeck, the brewer and banker.

Claypole

A mile to the east of the A1, and almost into Nottinghamshire, this peaceful village lies on the right bank of the Witham and has what Pevsner described as 'a proud church'. The

Ross Castle, on the seafront at Cleethorpes, is a folly built in 1885.

churchyard of St Peter's has some interesting gravestones too. The interior is of considerable architectural interest. There are also buildings along the village street worth admiring, including the Old Rectory (parts of which date back to the seventeenth century) situated at its far end. Equally venerable is the timber-framed row of Church View Cottages, which were encased in brick at a later date.

Cleethorpes
Early closing Thursday.
It is difficult to tell where Grimsby ends and Cleethorpes begins since they form a single conurbation along the south bank of the Humber estuary. Cleethorpes developed as a new village in the nineteenth century when the railway arrived in 1863, starting as a hamlet of the ancient village of Clee (now called Old Clee). Old Clee contains the venerable church of Holy Trinity with its Anglo-Saxon tower and rebuilt Saxon nave, where one pillar still records its consecration by St Hugh of Lincoln in 1192. Around the church are small red brick cottages with Dutch-style gable ends. Also in the vicinity is Clee Hall Farm, dating from the seventeenth century.

Cleethorpes Pier was opened on August Bank Holiday Monday 1873 at a cost of £10,000 and was then 1200 feet (366 metres) long. Two years later a landing stage was added to enable boat trips to run to Spurn Head lighthouse on the other side of the Humber. In 1940 much of the pier was blown up to discourage enemy landings there, resulting in the present truncated 335 feet (102 metres). To the east of the pier a folly known as Ross Castle was erected in 1885. The entrance to the Humber is marked by a pair of wartime forts.

Further along the shoreline are the Humberston Fitties, covered in sand dunes and caravans.

Jungle World, page 110.

In the locality: Scartho church, page 67; Waltham Tower Mill, page 107. See also Grimsby.

Colsterworth
Woolsthorpe Manor, page 92.

Coningsby
A large village on the edge of the Fens, it is not only the base for RAF Tornados and the Battle of Britain Memorial Flight but an

interesting place in its own right. The huge one-handed clock of St Michael's church is the largest such timepiece in Britain, with a dial measuring 16½ feet (5 metres) across. The tower itself has a processional way under it, which is very rare in the county. The war memorial beside the A153 takes the form of a polished granite shaft, which appears to have been sliced near its top to represent the cutting off of young lives in battle during the First World War – again unusual in Lincolnshire. The name of Gartree School is derived from the Danish wapentake name for this area.

Battle of Britain Memorial Flight Visitor Centre, page 94.

See also Tattershall and Tattershall Bridge.

Corby Glen

Corby Glen lies near the junction of the A151 and the B1176 to the south-east of Grantham. A former market town, it still has its market place, near which is the church of St John the Evangelist (a rare dedication in Lincolnshire). Its main attraction is the many medieval wall paintings that have been uncovered and preserved. These include an 11 feet (3.3 metres)

The clock face on St Michael's church, Coningsby, is the largest in Britain.

high figure of St Christopher, St Anne teaching her daughter the Virgin Mary, King Herod, the Magi and the Seven Deadly Sins, all favourite subjects for such murals. The former grammar school, now known as the Willoughby Memorial Art Gallery, was founded by Charles Read (whose name is honoured in the neighbouring secondary school) in 1673. A Latin inscription on the entablature records this event. The second part of the village's name, Glen, comes from the nearby river, which joins the Welland at Surfleet Seas End, near the Wash.

Its annual sheep fair is held in early October and dates from 1238.

Covenham St Bartholomew
Covenham Reservoir, page 109.

Cranwell
Cranwell Aviation Heritage Centre, page 94.

Crowland
Standing in the middle of the Fens at the southern boundary of Lincolnshire, the small town of Crowland is dominated by memories of its founder, St Guthlac. He was born in 667 and after a military career fighting for King Ethelred of Mercia he became a Benedictine monk, until he felt that God was calling him to found a hermitage in these then inaccessible fenlands. He drifted across the swamps in a small boat until his craft foundered on the shore of the island on which Crowland now stands. He died here in 714 after inviting his sister St Pega (from her cell at nearby Peakirk) to his funeral! An abbey was founded here in his honour in 716.

Worth a visit is the triangular Trinity Bridge. Dating from the fourteenth century, it stands on the site of an earlier bridge recorded in 943. Originally it stood over the confluence of two streams (hence its unique shape). The well worn figure on it has been variously identified as King Ethelred, the Virgin Mary and Christ. It is believed to have been removed from the west front of the abbey in about 1720.

There are some delightful little greens scattered round the town.

Crowland Abbey, page 68.

In the locality: Deeping St James church, page 75.

The medieval Trinity Bridge in Crowland formerly spanned a confluence of rivers.

The 1651 bridge over the river Welland at Deeping Gate.

Crowle
Early closing Wednesday; market day Friday.

Regarded as the 'northern capital' of the Isle of Axholme, Crowle lies on the busy twisting A161 road, which runs along the spine of the island, which was drained effectively in the first half of the seventeenth century by Sir Cornelius Vermuyden and his team of Dutch engineers.

Set off the main road is a quiet oasis around the ancient church of St Oswald, which is unusual in having separate roofs for the nave and chancel. Inside is the best Saxon cross in the area, covered in typical ropework patterns. On one side of it two figures are carved which are variously reported to represent St Paul talking to St Anthony or King Oswald and his brother Oswiu.

The centre of the town is attractive with its market place and hostelries.

In the locality: Sandtoft Transport Centre, page 99.

Croxton
Yarborough Camp, page 66.

Deeping St James
Lying on the edge of the small town of Market Deeping and on the banks of the river Welland, Deeping St James has an abbey church, but also two other ancient remains that are worth viewing. The first of these is the 1651 bridge over the river at that part of the village known as Deeping Gate. The other is near the church and was originally the market cross, dating from the fifteenth century. The shaft of the cross was destroyed when it was transformed into the village lock-up in 1819. Nowadays it serves yet another purpose, that of being the most unusual lamp post in Lincolnshire! Nearby are several interesting old houses and cottages, which give Deeping St James an old world charm.

Church of St James, page 75.

Doddington
Doddington Hall, page 83; Lincolnshire Road Transport Museum, page 97.

Donington
The 143 feet (43 metres) high steeple of the parish church of St Mary and the Holy Rood

The Old Rectory at Epworth, where John and Charles Wesley spent their childhood.

dominates this erstwhile market town, the birthplace of explorer Matthew Flinders (see page 114), whose monument is inside the church, as is a stained glass window recalling his exploits. Donington church (like nearby Pinchbeck) possesses a rare graveside shelter for the priest. The town has one of the oldest schools in the county – Cowley's (founded in 1719, and rebuilt after being gutted by fire in 1812). It faces a pleasant green, near King's Cross House, with its railwayana. There are still former coaching inns along the main streets, such as the Black Bull and the Red Cow, dating back in parts to the seventeenth century. There are examples of Georgian houses to admire.

Dorrington
North Ings Farm Museum, page 95.

East Kirkby
Lincolnshire Aviation Heritage Centre, page 95.

Edenham

This is an estate village for nearby Grimsthorpe Castle, and the cottages are in local Kesteven oolitic limestone, including the vicarage, portions of which date back to the seventeenth century. The Reverend Charles Kingsley lived in Edenham for a time, there writing both *The Water Babies* (1863) and *Hereward the Wake* (1866). In 1857 the then Lord Willoughby de Eresby opened his own little single-track railway to link the village with the East Coast main line at Little Bytham. Due to light ballasting and sharp curves there was an 8 mph (13 km/h) speed restriction. The line closed down in the early 1880s after horses had replaced the steam locomotives! The little booking office still stands by the site of the station beside the A151. St Michael's church contains many monuments to the owners of Grimsthorpe. It is built on a man-made platform that has yielded up Roman remains, and it contains some very early Saxon carvings.

Epworth

The 'southern capital' of the Isle of Axholme is on the island's highest incline. The main spine road, the A161, bisects the small town, renowned as the birthplace of John and Charles Wesley. In the Market Place stands the cross from the steps of which John preached, whilst staying at the Red Lion after the death of his father, Samuel, in 1735. Samuel Wesley had been Rector of Epworth since 1696, and St Andrew's church is to be found by going out of the Market Place up Church Street and then cutting down a tree-lined flagged path. His tomb is tucked in by the south wall of the church. To find the Old Rectory, where the Wesleys lived as children, go up Albion Hill and turn left into Rectory Street. Near the traffic lights on the A161 is the Wesley Memorial Church, opened in 1891 and containing a roundel depicting the two brothers in its east window.

The Old Rectory, page 86.

In the locality: Sandtoft Transport Centre, page 99.

Folkingham

In spite of being on the busy A15 Humber Bridge to Peterborough road, this former market town is well worth a visit.

From at least the seventeenth century until 1828 the Kesteven Quarter Sessions were held at the former Greyhound inn facing the large market square. Nearby, down Billingborough Road, was the house of correction, which was rebuilt in 1825, and of which only the forbidding entrance now remains. This institution was built on the site of a medieval castle, the moat of which survives.

Off the market square is St Andrew's church, the tower of which commands the surrounding undulating country of the Kesteven hills as they incline down towards the Fens. Inside the church are the village stocks.

In the locality: churches at Pickworth, page 80, and Sempringham, page 80.

Freiston

Church of St James, page 75.

Fulbeck

This fine-looking village is best summed up by Arthur Mee: 'Serene and fair to look upon it is, with houses nestling among fine old trees on the steep hillside.' The name itself means 'dirty brook'. As well as the elegant Perpendicular St Nicholas's church, the tower of which is crowned by eight pinnacles,

The house of correction at Folkingham is now one of the properties that can be rented from the Landmark Trust.

Fulbeck can also boast the venerable mansions Fulbeck House and Fulbeck Hall, both dating to the early eighteenth century. There is also, from the same period, the Manor House. The main village lies on the west side of the A607, and includes a craft centre with small workshops and a restaurant.
Fulbeck Hall, page 86.

Gainsborough
Early closing Wednesday; market days Tuesday and Saturday.
Gainsborough was reputedly 'St Oggs' in George Eliot's novel *The Mill on the Floss* (1860); the demolished Ashcroft Mill on the Trent waterfront was said to have been Eliot's model for Tulliver's mill. In the novel tragedy strikes with the onsurge of the eagre (or aeger), the tidal bore that takes its name from the Danish god Oegir the Terrible. Normally this happens fifty minutes after high tide in the Humber at Grimsby and it can be between 8 feet (2.5 metres) and 13 feet (4 metres) high. Times are given in the local press.

The Danes came here in force under King Sweyne Forkbeard, who died at Gainsborough in 1014 and was buried temporarily at Castle Hills above the town.

There was a ferry across the Trent until 1791, when Gainsborough Bridge was built. It is still basically the same although it was tastefully widened in 1964.

All Saints' church has a 90 feet (27 metres) high Perpendicular tower, but the rest of the building consists of the only Georgian town church in Lincolnshire, dating from 1736-42.

Nearby is Gainsborough Old Hall. A contrasting building, which played an essential part in the development of the town in the nineteenth century, is the Britannia Works of William Marshall & Sons in Beaumont Street. The earliest part dates from 1850 and the main entrance is surmounted by a fine figure of Britannia.

Gainsborough Old Hall, page 87; **Britannia Works**, page 103.

In the locality: churches at Marton, page 79, and Stow, page 80; Bomber County Aviation Museum, page 97.

Gedney
Church of St Mary Magdalene, page 75.

Goulceby
Red Hill, page 63.

Goxhill
Situated on the Humber Bank to the northeast of Barrow-upon-Humber, this large village used to flourish from passing traffic on its way to and from a ferry that crossed the river between Goxhill Ferry and Hull. The former ferry terminal stands at the most northerly point of the old Lincolnshire.

There are many interesting and elegant houses in the village centre, clustered around the church of All Saints, built in the Early English style. In the south porch (now reached only from the interior of the church) is a mid fifteenth-century painting of the Crucifixion.

At South End, Goxhill, is Goxhill Priory, adjoining a handsome house of about 1700. There are no monastic connections, however, for the so-called 'Priory' is a late fourteenth-century domestic building, with a fine ribbed undercroft, where ashlar and brick have been placed next to one another. This part has been excavated. The Priory is not open to the public but can be admired from the road.

A collection of railway models, tickets and other relics can be visited at Goxhill Railway Centre at Goxhill railway station, still served by trains between Cleethorpes and Barton-upon-Humber.

In the locality: Thornton Abbey, page 72.

Grantham
Early closing Wednesday; market day Saturday.
The crowning glory of this busy engineering town on the upper reaches of the river Witham is St Wulfram's church, its spire a landmark to road and rail travellers passing through Grantham. The Beehive inn in Castlegate, near the church, has a living sign, a real beehive outside the public house. Opposite St Wulfram's is the oldest building of King's School, founded under Edward IV (who gave the town its charter in 1464) by Bishop Richard Fox, born in nearby Ropsley. Amongst its famous pupils were William

Cecil (later Lord Burghley) and Sir Isaac Newton, whose statue by William Theed the Younger stands on St Peter's Hill outside the French-styled Guildhall of 1867-9. Another former pupil was the seventeenth-century theologian, philosopher and hymn writer Henry More.

The former Prime Minister Baroness Thatcher was born Margaret Roberts in the town in 1925. She attended the Grantham and Kesteven Girls' High School. The general store her father owned in Broad Street has been a restaurant and a chiropodist's but its future is uncertain.

Many famous travellers have stayed at the Angel and Royal Hotel in High Street. It was originally the property of the Knights Templars and after their disgrace was handed over to the Hospitallers. The present front was built in the fifteenth century and has the eroded heads of Edward III and Queen Philippa on its archway. In 1483 Richard III signed the death warrant of the second Duke of Buckingham here. At the rear is a long

brick range dated to 1776. Round the corner is Vine Street with Vine House of 1764.

In the Market Place stand the plinth of a medieval cross and the town's conduit of 1597 (similar to one in Lincoln).

Grantham still abounds in 'blue' pub names and street names: the old slate title plates can be deciphered at the entrances to Guildhall Street, Union Street and Welby Street. John Manners, Earl of Dysart, who purchased the

Grantham still has its town conduit (right), erected in 1597, and (below) its famous inn, the Angel and Royal, shown here decorated with a Christmas angel.

The Dock Tower at Grimsby was built by William Armstrong, the hydraulic engineer, and held a water tank of 33,000 gallons (150,000 litres).

manor of Grantham, decided to rename inns to reflect his Whig allegiance (the party colour was blue).

Wharf Road is a reminder that Grantham was the terminus of a canal to Nottingham from 1797 to 1936. Now it is the site of the Sir Isaac Newton Shopping Centre, built in 1983.

St Mary's Catholic church, page 76; **church of St Wulfram**, page 77; **Finkin Street Methodist church**, page 77; **Grantham House**, page 90; **Grantham Museum**, page 95.

In the locality: Belton House, page 82; Geeson Bros Motorcycle Museum, page 99; Harlaxton Manor and Gardens, page 91; Marston Hall and Gardens, page 92.

Grimsby

Early closing Thursday; market days Tuesday, Friday and Saturday.

Until 1848 Grimsby was an ancient but small port, which was not even one of the ten lar-

gest towns in Lincolnshire in 1801. Yet by 1901 it ranked second only to Lincoln and was soon to outstrip the county town in size. The key to the town's growth was the arrival of the railway, which enabled fish to be transported fast and in vast quantities to all parts of Britain. New docks were built, and they were connected with the river Humber by lock gates operated hydraulically from the 303 feet (92 metres) high Dock Tower. As well as commercial docks, three fish docks covering 63 acres (25.5 hectares) were excavated. By 1927 there were over seven hundred trawlers operating out of these docks, but by the early 1980s there had been a dramatic fall in the number of vessels sailing out of Grimsby to fish, and now part of the fish docks is being converted into a yacht marina.

Grim (originally another name for the Norse god Odin) was said to have been a local fisherman, who rescued the son of Kirk Birkabeen of Denmark, and a statue outside the College of Technology shows Grim with the young Havelok on his shoulders.

Many nineteenth-century and earlier buildings have been swept away to make room for Freshney Place and other modern developments, but the imposing Town Hall of 1863 has been spared. The new Grimsby Auditorium opened in 1995.

Worth a detour from the town centre is the People's Park along Welholme Road. Opened in 1883, it covers 27 acres (10.9 hectares).

The paddle steamer *Lincoln Castle* in the Alexandra Dock serves refreshments next to the National Fishing Heritage Centre.

National Fishing Heritage Centre, page 95; **Grimsby Dock Tower**, page 103; **Victoria Mill**, page 103; **Freshney Park Way**, page 110.

See also Cleethorpes.

Grimsthorpe

Grimsthorpe Castle, page 90.

Gunby

Gunby Hall, page 90.

Harlaxton

Harlaxton Manor, page 91; Harlaxton Manor Gardens, page 91.

Hatcliffe

This small village down country lanes off the A18 at the northern end of the Wolds has a little stream running beside its main street, crossed by innumerable small brick bridges, making a picturesque scene. St Mary's church stands on a bank and is principally constructed in local ironstone, dating from the thirteenth century, but with a nineteenth-century chancel. Along Barton Street (which has prehistoric origins, albeit now the A18) stands a watermill, in a dip in the road, dating from 1774, and possessing a Yorkshire flagstone roof.

Haxey

Haxey Hood Game, page 120.

Heckington

The 182 feet (55 metres) high steeple of St Andrew's church can be seen for miles across the surrounding Fens. Its greatest claims to fame are its rare Easter sepulchre and its massive seven-light window. Now that the A17 bypasses the village, the visitor can examine the many interesting houses with much more ease. The almshouses on the green date from 1886 and are in memory of Henry Godson; they are matched by a similar group

The Pea Room at Heckington.

dedicated to Edward Godson situated to the north-east of the church and dating from 1904. Both are Gothic in concept.

A walk down to the railway station is well worth while for three reasons: there is a small museum on the platform; nearby are the eight-sailed windmill and also the Pea Room (now a craft centre).

Church of St Andrew, page 77; **tower mill**, page 103.

In the locality: South Kyme Priory, page 70; Helpringham church, page 77; Scredington packhorse bridge, page 69.

Helpringham

Church of St Andrew, page 77.

Hemswell

Bomber County Aviation Museum, page 97.

Holbeach

Early closing Wednesday; market day Thursday.

In the middle of the Fens, in what used to be Parts of Holland, stands this small market town set in one of the largest parishes in England, 15 miles (24 km) from one end to the other and covering 21,000 acres (8500 hectares). It is the centre for such hamlets as Holbeach St Mat-

thew, Holbeach St Mark, Hobeach St Luke (or Holbeach Bank), Holbeach St John, Holbeach Clough (pronounced to rhyme with 'cow') and Holbeach Drove.

All Saints' church with its 180 feet (55 metres) high spire can be seen for miles. Its entrance porch is said to have come from neighbouring Moulton Castle. Inside there are brasses to Joanna Welbye (died 1488) and a headless knight (c.1420). There is also a fine effigy of Sir Humphrey Littlebury (c. 1400).

Along the High Street is the imposing Mansion House where Sir Norman Angell (Lane) was born in 1872. He became the editor and author of books on international affairs, which won him the Nobel Peace Prize in 1933. The antiquarian Dr William Stukeley (see page 117) was born in a house Barrington Gate. Stukeley Hall (built in 1922) along the Spalding road was named after him. Further along that road there is a millstone placed on the Greenwich Meridian and also celebrating the Coronation of Elizabeth II in 1953.

In the locality: Gedney church, page 75.

Horncastle

Early closing Wednesday; market days
Thursday and Saturday.

Horncastle takes its name from the fact that a Roman *castra* (literally a 'camp', but in this case a posting station) was founded at the confluence of the small rivers Bain and Waring, which join in the shape of a pair of horns as seen on prehistoric cattle. In the fourth century walls were built to enclose the 7 acre (2.8 hectare) site, and fragments of these can still be seen to the south of St Mary's church and in the public library in Riverside.

St Mary's has a diminutive spire on its tower, the lower half of which is in the Early English style and the top half in that of the Decorated period. Beside the north porch is the flat tombstone of a nineteenth-century local doctor, who wished to be buried in unhallowed ground in order to identify himself with suicides he had known. It has since lost its vertical cross. Inside St Mary's on the north aisle wall is a brass portrait of Lionel Dymoke (1519), a member of the family of the hereditary King's Champions from the nearby village of Scrivelsby. Over the arch in the south aisle are thirteen scythe blades said to have been used in the Lincolnshire Rising of October 1536, when the bishop's chancellor, Dr Raynes, was clubbed to death on the nearby Wong (water meadow on the banks of the Waring). On 11th October 1643 Sir Ingram Hopton, a Royalist commander, was defeated and killed at the battle of Winceby. The site is at the junction of the A158 and B1195 roads several miles to the east of the town. He was given a military funeral by the Parliamentarian forces and his memorial hangs on the south aisle wall of the church. Nearby are Ingram Street and Hopton Street.

In Church Lane is the tiny cobbler's shop of William Marwood, who was public hangman, 1872-83.

In the Market Place is the Gothic monument to the Right Honourable E. Stanhope, who was Conservative member of Parliament for Horncastle from the establishment of the constituency in 1885 until his death in 1894. The dark red brick house on the south-east corner of the Market Place was the town house of the notable botanist Sir Joseph Banks (of Botany Bay fame), whose country mansion was Revesby Abbey. Banks Street, beside the Horncastle Navigation canal, is named in his honour. This canal was supported by Sir Joseph, who arranged for its route to be surveyed between the town and the river Witham near Tattershall in 1791. The canal opened in 1802 and was operational until 1878.

Number 30 South Street, a house on the west side, has a death mask over the doorway. This is of so-called 'Tiger Tom', who was executed in 1829 for robbery.

In the locality: Red Hill, page 63; Snipe Dales Country Park, page 60; Tupholme Abbey, page 73.

Hough-on-the-Hill

This small upland Kesteven village has one of the finest examples of Anglo-Saxon architecture in the lower section of the west tower of All Saints' church. Pevsner equates it in quality to the more famous Northamptonshire churches at Brixworth and

Brigstock. The tower has a semicircular stair projection, which is unique in Lincolnshire. There are earlier examples of Anglo-Saxon work in the nave. Nearby is the little hamlet of Gelston, overlooking the Witham valley, with its medieval cross on its diminutive green.

Immingham
Early closing Wednesday.
Immingham was a small village until work began on the docks in 1904. Its ancient nucleus was inland around the parish church of St Andrew, parts of which date back to the Norman period. Near the church is the Bluestone Inn, in the forecourt of which stands a large glacial erratic boulder, which once stood nearer the Humber Bank. In 1607 a group of Puritans from north Lincolnshire, Nottinghamshire and Yorkshire sailed from the shore at Immingham to the Netherlands. In 1925 a 20 foot (6 metre) column on a plinth of granite from the famous Plymouth Rock was erected by the Anglo-American Society to commemorate this event.

King George V opened the Immingham Docks in 1912 and as a consequence the Great Central Railway switched its passenger liner service to Scandinavia from Grimsby to the new facilities. At the same time the Great Central built a network of railway lines to serve the port. The imposing County Hotel was opened on the site of the shanty town of construction workers' huts. With the opening of the Lindsey Oil Refinery in neighbouring Killingholme in 1968, the Humber had to be dredged to take the huge modern tankers. This enabled further expansion at Immingham, including the National Coal Board terminal (1970) and that of British Steel (1972). Passenger services ceased in 1977 when Tor Line transferred its operations to Felixstowe.

In the modern centre of Immingham stands the Kennedy Way shopping precinct, opened in 1966.
Immingham Museum, page 97.
In the locality: Thornton Abbey, page 72.

Ingoldmells
Hardy's Animal Farm, page 110.

Kirkstead
Kirkstead Abbey, page 68.

Kirton-in-Holland
This large Fenland village stands on the A16 to the south of Boston. Sir Nikolaus Pevsner described the King's Head of 1699 as an example of 'Fen Artisan Mannerism', being in brick with window sills that almost touch the pavement outside. Opposite is the handsome parish church of Saints Peter and Paul with its Perpendicular-style central tower, which was rebuilt in 1805. The Norman interior was restored in 1900. Kirton-in-Holland was once a small market town, as the space between the church and the former King's Head indicates. Near the Town Hall (1911) stands Lindley Clark's statue of William Dennis, a local benefactor.

Kirton-in-Lindsey
This small town was the site of both the Lindsey Quarter Sessions and Lindsey's house of correction from 1791 until 1868 and 1872 respectively. Nothing remains of the former bridewell. The Town Hall of 1887 presides over an irregular network of narrow streets running off the former Market Place.

St Andrew's church is an impressive sight on its considerable mound at the western end of Kirton, where there is a steep slope down towards the valley of the river Eau and the Gainsborough to Brigg railway line. Parts of it, including the priest's doorway in the chancel, are Norman, but much of the church, including the massive tower, dates from the thirteenth century. Opposite the church is a pleasing terrace of early brick cottages.

To the north of Kirton is Mount Pleasant windmill, now without sails.
Mount Pleasant Windmill, page 103; **St Andrew's bells**, page 120.

Langtoft
Fenland Aquajets, page 110.

Langton-by-Partney
Church of St Peter and St Paul, page 78.

Langworth
Langworth Animal Park, page 111.

Leadenham

For many years known as Long Leadenham, this important stone-built village stands at the crossroads of the A607 and the former A17, halfway up Lincoln Cliff, and overlooking the Trent flood plain. In 1839 a cutting was made to ease the climb for stage-coaches up to the village, but it still left a 10 per cent hill leading up to the two Georgian hostelries, the Feathers and the George. As well as a pleasing collection of houses, Leadenham possesses an imposing church, dedicated to St Swithin. In 1841 the artist and architect Augustus Pugin, aged twenty-nine, painted the chancel ceiling in a flamboyant style.

Legbourne

Legbourne Railway Museum, page 97.

Lincoln

A walk round Lincoln city centre

Warning: since it is not possible to visit most of the places listed below without climbing steep hills, those with disabilities may be advised to avoid the complete route.

Start at **St Mary's Conduit** (of 1540) by the High Street level crossing. Next to this is the ancient church of **St Mary-le-Wigford**, one of the few survivors of the forty-five churches that were to be found in medieval Lincoln. It has a Saxon-Norman tower, is the base for a team ministry and sometimes houses art and other exhibitions. Above this point High Street is pedestrianised. **St Benedict's Square** is centred around another of the extant medieval churches, but only the chancel and a north chapel of St Benedict's date to that period. It is now the Mothers' Union church and refreshments can be obtained there. On **High Bridge** over the river Witham, before its widening, there was a chapel dedicated to St Thomas of Canterbury. However, it does still possess the **High Bridge Café**, the sides of which contain sixteenth-century beams, although the front was reconstructed in 1900-1. Under it the passage of the Witham is known locally as 'Glory Hole'. The **Waterside Centre** shopping precinct dates only from 1990. Ahead stands the **Stonebow**, the late medieval gateway into the old city, and completed in 1520 with the guildhall above it.

Further along High Street, on the corner of Grantham Street is the **Cardinal's Hat**, dating from the late fifteenth century and restored in 1952-3. It is named in honour of Cardinal Thomas Wolsey, who was briefly Bishop of Lincoln in 1514. **Strait** has the same derivation as the street in Damascus mentioned in the Acts of the Apostles, meaning 'narrow'. Where it ends and becomes Steep Hill, at its junction with Danes Terrace, are two Norman town houses, known as **Jews House** and **Jews Court**. There was a thriving Jewish community in the city until a persecution following the death of Little St Hugh in 1225. He was said, falsely, to have been murdered by Jews and his body dumped down a local well.

Christ's Hospital Terrace enables the visitor to turn into the churchyard of **St Michael-on-the-Mount** (rebuilt in 1855-6) for a panoramic view over the lower city with its complex of engineering works and James Fowler's magnificent St Swithin's church (rebuilt on a new site, 1869-87). The junction of Steep Hill and Michaelgate marks the site of the former Fish Shambles. On the corner of Christ's Hospital Terrace stands another Norman house, wrongly in the past called the house of **Aaron the Jew**, although he was well-known as a rich moneylender *c.*1170.

At the top of Steep Hill is the timber-framed **Leigh-Pemberton House**, flanked on one side by the barbican of Lincoln Castle and on the other side by the medieval Exchequer Gate, beyond which is the Cathedral. Also on Castle Hill is the small church of **St Mary Magdalene**, last rebuilt in 1882. Past Gordon Road, set in the middle of Bailgate, are cobbles marking the positions of the columns of a colonade of the large basilica in the **Roman Forum**. Also dating from that period is a well near the end of Westgate, along with the outline of Lincoln's first Christian church of **St Paul-in-the-Bail**, which was excavated when the last Victorian church on the site was demolished.

Enter West Bight and behind the Castle Hotel is the **Mint Wall**. This is thought to be part of the wall of the Roman basilica and still stands some 20 feet (6 metres) tall. **Newport**

Jew's House and Jew's Court, Lincoln.

The Lucy Tower and ramparts at Lincoln Castle.

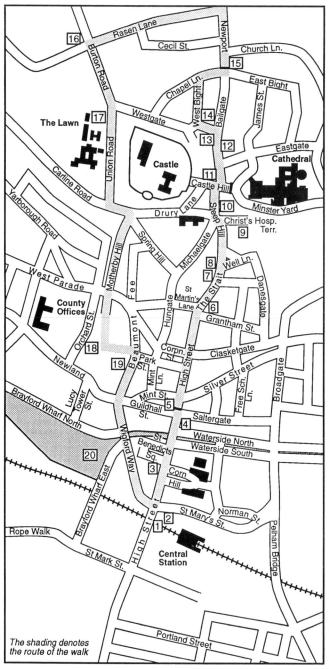

Street plan of Lincoln, showing the route of the suggested walk. Key: 1 St Mary's Conduit; 2 St Mary-le-Wigford church; 3 St Benedict's church; 4 Waterside Centre; 5 Stonebow; 6 Cardinal's Hat; 7 Jew's House; 8 Jew's Court; 9 St Michael-on-the-Mount; 10 Aaron the Jew's House; 11 Leigh-Pemberton House; 12 colonnade of basilica; 13 Roman well and St Paul-in-the-Bail church; 14 Mint Wall; 15 Newport Arch; 16 Museum of Lincolnshire Life; 17 The Lawn; 18 lower gateway, Roman city; 19 site of St Mary Crackpole church and Friends' Meeting House; 20 Brayford Pool.

The sixteenth-century Leigh-Pemberton House in Lincoln.

Arch is the sole surviving Roman gateway in Britain that is still in use for traffic and was the northern entrance into the Roman garrison.

At the far end of Rasen Lane, at the crossroads are the Old Barracks, which now house the **Museum of Lincolnshire Life**. On the east side of Union Road stands the recently excavated and restored West Gate into the Castle, whilst on the west side is **The Lawn**. Built as a lunatic asylum in 1819-20, in recent years it has been converted to a multitude of uses. These include an exhibition showing how the treatment of mental illnesses has changed over the centuries, the National Cycle Museum, and in the former swimming pool a collection of tropical trees and plants connected with the life of Sir Joseph Banks (see page 114).

At the foot of Union Road, note the danger warning at the top of Spring Hill, before crossing to descend the steep pedestrianised Motherby Hill (unmarked). This runs beside the western wall of the Roman city. Cross over West Parade and down a cul-de-sac to a footpath that leads to the remains of the **Lower West Gate** of the Roman city. This was excavated when the County Offices were being built. Cross the adjacent car park into **Beaumont Fee** (named after the nearby manor owned by the Beaumont family until 1507). The churchyard on its corner belonged to the long-gone church of St Mary Crackpole. At its southern end stands the **Friends' Meeting House**, parts of which date back to 1689, the year of the Toleration Act.

Wigford Way gives the visitor a good view of the expanse of **Brayford Pool**, where the river Witham and the Roman canal, the Fossdyke, meet. The name 'Lincoln' is derived from the Latin words *Lindis Colonia*, meaning the colony of ex-servicemen by the water (Brayford Pool).

Other places to visit in Lincoln include the Roman East Gate (page 66), St Mary's medieval Guildhall and the Saxo-Norman St Peter-at-Gowts along High Street on the other side of the railway crossing. Off Monks Road are the Arboretum (established in 1872) and the roofless cell of a daughter house of St Mary's Abbey, York.

Louth Market Place on a summer Wednesday.

Little Bytham

Londonthorpe

Situated on the eastern lip of the upper Witham valley within viewing distance of Grantham, this is typical of several oolitic limestone estate villages that surround that town. The village's name has nothing to do with the capital city, but was originally 'Lundertorp' ('the settlement by the grove'). The trees have mostly disappeared, but this is still a very attractive little community. The church of St John the Baptist has a rare saddleback roof tower of possibly twelfth-century date, while the rest of the building is probably from the following century. The tower is mirrored in one of the buildings of Manor Farm at the back of the conduit house, restored as a bus shelter!

Long Bennington

Until the 1960s the A1 passed through this straggling village, which stretches for over a mile (1.6 km). Since the opening of the bypass Long Bennington can be enjoyed by those wanting to see its interesting buildings. These are as varied as the 'tin' church and hall of St James (1890), the bow-windowed Royal Oak and the Georgian Priory House (a reminder that in the middle ages the village contained a small cell belonging to the abbey of Sevigney in Normandy). At the southern end of Long Bennington stands St Swithin's parish church, with its unusually shaped 1977 Silver Jubilee clock and two pieces of modern art inside depicting the Nativity and Crucifixion.

Donkeys on the sands at Mablethorpe.

Long Sutton

Early closing Wednesday; market day Friday.

The crowning glory of this little market town is the *lead* spire of St Mary's church, which reaches a height of 162 feet (49 metres), the ninth highest in the county. It is the oldest such spire in England, dating from the thirteenth century. It was used as a seamark by mariners on the Wash for centuries. The double-decker porch of the fifteenth century and the two-storeyed 'vestiarium' in the north-east corner of the church are both worth visiting. The upper room of the porch was used as a schoolroom at one time. In the Market Place is the town pump in its wooden case, bearing the arms of the former Long Sutton Urban District Council. A butterfly park opened in 1986.

Butterfly and Falconry Park, page 109.

In the locality: Gedney church, page 75; Museum of Entertainment, page 100.

Louth

Early closing Thursday; market days Wednesday, Friday and Saturday.

The enormous and elegant parish church of St James has the tallest spire on any English parish church (295 feet or 90 metres). To the west of it is Westgate with its Georgian houses having a variety of wooden porches; amongst them is the low-roofed Wheatsheaf inn of an earlier period. Down a side alley on the north side, Westgate Place, leading down towards the river Lud, is the house where Alfred Tennyson lodged while a pupil at the King Edward VI School. At the far end of Westgate, by the bridge over the Lud, there is a fine view of The Cedars, the birthplace of Charlotte Allington Pye in 1830. Under the pseudonym 'Claribel', she became a popular composer of ballads, including 'You and I' and 'Maggie's Secret'. After her death in 1869 a memorial window to her was installed at the west end of St James's.

In Bridge Street a splendid Regency terrace has been beautifully restored. On the side of the town watermill, designed by Francis Julien in 1755, is one of several flood level marks, which record how far the Lud rose during the flash flood of 29th May 1920, caused by a cloudburst over the Wolds to the west of the town. In that deluge and subsequent inundation twenty-three men, women and children were drowned. There is a monument to them in the cemetery in London Road. Opposite the mill is the former churchyard of Louth's original parish church, St Mary's.

Down Little Eastgate is the imposing Town Hall of 1854, opposite the fine Market Hall of 1866 with its tall tower. Nearby stands the former Wesleyan Centenary Church of 1835; although externally only slightly modified, it was completely transformed internally as Louth Methodist Church in 1977.

Beside the Town Hall, Cannon Street contains the Playhouse cinema, which was once the Congregational church.

Along Upgate stands the Mansion House (once the public library), of the late eighteenth century. On the corner of Upgate and Mercer Row is Cromwell House (a restaurant), a sixteenth-century timber-framed building, like several others in the vicinity which are now disguised behind more modern façades. In the Cornmarket auctions take place every Wednesday lunchtime, in addition to the normal street markets, held on Fridays and Saturdays.

At the eastern end of Louth lies the former hamlet of Riverhead grouped round the canal basin, which has been landscaped and provided with Muscovy ducks. The Louth Navigation, designed by John Grundy, the Spalding engineer, was operational between 1767 and 1924, and linked the town with the North Sea at Tetney Haven, using the water of the Lud. The locks were of a unique design: instead of the sides being parallel, they consisted of four segmental arches curved into the land. Some warehousing remains.

Church of St James, page 79; **Methodist church**, page 79; **Louth Museum**, page 98; **Louth Riverhead**, page 105; **Eve's Carpet Factory**, page 104; **Kids Kingdom**, page 111.

In the locality: Hubbard's Hill, page 60; Legbourne Railway Museum, page 97; Alvingham Mill, page 101; Utterby packhorse bridge, page 73.

Ludford

The village sign claims Ludford to be of Danish origins. Although its name suggests that

the river Lud flows through it en route to Louth, the river here is the Bain, beginning its journey towards Horncastle! For many centuries the village consisted of two separate manors: Ludford Magna and Ludford Parva. Today it is one linear settlement joined by Magna Mile (the A631). The two churches have been replaced by the 1863 building dedicated to St Mary and St Peter, which was designed by James Fowler of Louth.

Lutton

In past centuries this village was sometimes referred to as Sutton St Nicholas. The name Lutton is derived from words meaning 'the settlement by the pool'.

Situated in the heart of the southern Holland Fens to the north of Long Sutton, the village's focal point is the tall spire of St Nicholas's church, the top of which reaches a height of 159 feet (48 metres) – the twelfth tallest in Lincolnshire. The present church is in the Perpendicular style and is largely built of brick, as is virtually everything else in this stoneless and naturally treeless area. Inside, near the pulpit, is a portrait of a grim-looking Dr Richard Busby, who was born in the village in 1605 and won a scholarship to Westminster School, where he became headmaster for a record period of over fifty years. He also invented a universal phonetic alphabet of thirty-six letters.

Opposite the church is the Jolly Crispin pub, named after the patron saint of shoemakers, martyred with his brother Crispinian by the Emperor Diocletian in 259. At the other end of the village a former Methodist chapel has been converted into the workshop of Martin Vestments, for making clerical garments.

Mablethorpe
Early closing Thursday.
Much of the original village has long since disappeared under the waves of the North Sea, including St Peter's, the second parish church. St Mary's still stands but was extensively rebuilt in the seventeenth and early eighteenth centuries, using brick, because of the local scarcity of suitable stone. The church contains the brass memorial of Elizabeth Fitzwilliam, who lived at Mablethorpe Hall

and who died in 1522. This building stands near the junction of the A1104 and A1031. The Park Sports Centre was opened in 1986 next to the open air market, on the site of the former railway station. On 31st January 1953 the town centre was badly affected by the disastrous North Sea floods.
North End Animal Gardens, page 111.

Market Deeping

Built where the A15 crosses the river Welland and the A16, this small town serves a large area of the southern Lincolnshire Fens. The market place has become a car park but Market Deeping flourishes as a commuter village for Peterborough. Almost jutting into the A15, St Guthlac's is basically a Perpendicular-style church with earlier parts inside. Also dating from the middle ages is the Rectory. In the Market Place the stone-built Deeping Stage inn dates only from 1802, although it appears to be much older. Along the A16 Stamford road is a very attractive watermill, three storeys high and with a striking wooden porch looking out on to a hanging garden.

Market Rasen

Early closing Thursday; market day Tuesday.
Although now bypassed by the A46, Market Rasen is still on the busy holiday route of the A631. It stands at the western foot of the Wolds and on the banks of the diminutive river Rase, a tributary of the Ancholme. Its weekly market has shrunk in size, but the town is still the railhead for places as far away as Louth. A dozen horse-race meetings a year, including ones on Easter Monday and Boxing Day, are held at the modern course to the east of the town, which is one of the best small racecourses and is very popular with families. Amongst other amenities, there is a picnic area in the middle of the course.

St Thomas's church has a typical local ironstone tower of the early fifteenth century. It contains a modern font and a charming modern stained glass window depicting the Nativity. In 1599 its vicar, William Storr, was murdered outside by Francis Cartwright, only son of the lord of the manor, after he had taken the side of the poor against Cartwright's

father. Near the railway station (of 1848) stands the impressive Centenary Methodist Church of 1863 with its Ionic portico and pediment.
Centenary Wesleyan church, page 79.
In the locality: West Rasen packhorse bridge, page 73.

Marston

Marston Hall and Gardens, page 92.

Marton

Church of St Margaret, page 79.

Metheringham

Airfield Visitor Centre, page 98.

Moulton

The main village of this extensive Fenland parish is an oasis of treelined roads and parkland, just off the A151 Spalding to Holbeach road. Its foci are the mill tower and the church. The former of brick (*c.*1822) stands 97 feet (29 metres) high and was described by Pevsner as 'looking like a giraffe'! All Saints' church's steeple measures 165 feet (50 metres), in contrast. At one time Moulton could boast of a castle and, until the pupils were transferred to Spalding, a grammar school. There are some fine buildings, including town-style houses along High Street, such as Harrox House, Bayfield and Mill House. On the other side of the A151 down a narrow lane is the Elloe stone.
In the locality: Elloe Stone, page 67.

Navenby

The wide main street (now the A607) of this Lincoln Cliff village was once the site of a small market. Church Lane leads off this beside the Georgian Butchers' Arms to St Peter's church, which, although much altered over the centuries, still retains its Easter sepulchre. From the church views over the Witham and Brant valley can be obtained.

New Bolingbroke

The Crescent, page 105.

New Holland

The ferry crossing of the Humber between New Holland and Hull started in the days of

Seals at Donna Nook on the coast near North Somercotes.
                              Opposite: Medlam Drain by Frithville, north of Boston.
Orchids flowering at the Lincolnshire Trust reserve at Rimac near Saltfleet.

stage-coaches, being a shorter route than the earlier one from Barton-upon-Humber. However, it was the arrival of the railway here in 1848 that led to the growth of the modern village, dominated by the Lincoln Castle hotel, named after the last of the paddle steamers to ply as a Humber ferry, and which is now moored at Grimsby. Formerly this hotel was called the Yarborough Arms in honour of the chairman of the Manchester, Sheffield & Lincolnshire Railway Company, which constructed the 1375 foot (420 metre) pier that carried the trains out to New Holland Pier station and the huge 500 ton floating pontoon (the largest in Britain when it was opened). But on 24th June 1981 the ferryboat service ceased with the opening of the Humber Bridge. Also deriving its name from the railway company is Manchester Square, with its attractively restored workers' houses. Christ Church, the red brick parish church, was built in 1901.

Manchester Square, page 105.

Normanby

Normanby Hall and Country Park, page 92; Normanby Park Farming Museum, page 93.

North Thoresby

The central point of this commuter village for Louth and Grimsby is The Square, a triangular T junction, with a rebuilt mud and stud thatched cottage on one side. Originally this had two storeys, until gutted by a fire and substantially rebuilt in 1993. Down the narrow lane leading off The Square stands St Helen's church, connected with the ecclesiastical architect and historian Francis Bond, who was born locally in 1850. The Methodist chapel had the village school joined on to it (a rare survivor of Methodist schools in Lincolnshire) until a new school was built nearby in 1985.

In the locality: Covenham Reservoir, page 109.

Old Bolingbroke

Bolingbroke Castle, page 68.

Old Leake

This is the main settlement of a large marshland parish that also contains the satellite communities of New Leake and Leake Commonside. It owes its prosperity to growing potatoes and cabbages in its rich soil. St Mary's church, with its low sixteenth-century tower, is almost unaltered since medieval times. Inside there is a fifteenth-century alabaster effigy of a knight. The church is approached through a fine example of a lychgate. On the opposite side of the road the village stores still has early twentieth-century farmworkers' boots hanging from hooks in its ceiling with pre-1920 price tags affixed to them! Old Leake is a peaceful haven now that the busy holiday route, the A52, has been taken along a bypass.

Osbournby

Situated beside the A15 and just to the north of the A52, Osbournby (pronounced 'Ozemby') lies in undulating Kesteven hill country south of Sleaford. Once there were two public houses and several shops grouped round a triangular village green. The hostelries and most of the shops have gone now, and the green has been tarmacked to provide more car-parking space. However, this is still a picturesque village to stroll around. By the A15 is the former school, erected in 1846 of good local stone. Next to it is the parish church of Saints Peter and Paul, mainly of the Decorated period. Its principal treasures are its carved bench ends, many of which have interesting scenes illustrating medieval life, including a fine one depicting St George slaying the dragon. There are several attractive houses in the village, including Osbournby Hall down West Street.

On the second weekend in July each year the villagers hold their Feast, which dates back at least to the eighteenth century, although not now run on such a grand scale as it once was. Nevertheless a Lincolnshire delicacy, stuffed chine, is still served during the Saturday.

Oxcombe

The tiny hamlet of Oxcombe is a sanctuary of peace. It is situated in a small dry valley below the ancient ridgeway called the Bluestone Heath Road, which joins the A153 near Cadwell Park and the A16 near Swaby.

Down a steep narrow lane the driver comes to All Saints' church (1842) and Oxcombe House (1845), both designed by the Lincoln architect W. A. Nicholson to fit into the back-cloth of the Wolds.

Partney

Situated at the junction of the A16 and A158, Partney used to be reached by small craft sailing up the river Lymm many centuries ago, when the water table was higher. The parish church, with its handsome greenstone medieval tower, is dedicated to St Nicholas, the patron saint of sailors. The ship weathervane, however, celebrates a much later association with the sea, when the Australian explorer Matthew Flinders was married here. The brick chancel of the church dates from 1828. Near the church (along the A16) is a charming row of cottages, once thatched, but now pantiled. In a field beside the A158 the annual Sheep Fair is still held, as it has been for hundreds of years.

Pickworth

Church of St Andrew, page 80.

Ropsley

St Peter's church is mentioned by name in the Domesday Book (it is rare for dedications to be so listed), and it still has its Anglo-Saxon nave. The Early English tower is surmounted by a Decorated broach spire like so many other parish churches in this part of the former Parts of Kesteven. This large stone village lies to the east of Grantham and was the birthplace of Richard Fox (*c.* 1448), who, as well as founding Corpus Christi College, Oxford, also established the King's School in Grantham. He worked closely with Henry VII, both before and after he ascended the throne in 1485, retiring from affairs of state in 1516, but remaining Bishop of Winchester until his death in 1528. His birthplace can still be seen along the village's main street.

Saltfleet and Skidbrook

Saltfleet has had a chequered history. In the middle ages it was a flourishing port and had a market. Then, in the reign of Charles II, it became Lincolnshire's first seaside resort with

the erection of the New Inn for such visitors. Its own church (St John the Baptist) was swallowed up by the sea centuries ago, and until its village school was converted into a place of worship in the twentieth century the inhabitants had to cross the fields to St Botolph's, Skidbrook (a name meaning dirty stream). This was closed in 1973, restored and then placed into the hands of the Redundant Churches Fund. The old cottages in front of the Methodist church in Saltfleet were demolished in 1990 and their site laid out as a peaceful public garden, away from the holiday traffic on the A1031. The Rimac nature reserve is nearby.

In the locality: Donna Nook Nature Reserve, page 61.

Sandtoft

Sandtoft Transport Centre, page 99;
Sandtoft Gathering, page 121.

Saxilby

This large commuter village near Lincoln stands on the north bank of the Roman Fossdyke canal, halfway between Brayford Pool (Lincoln) and Torksey Lock on the Trent. Nowadays the canal is used almost entirely by pleasure craft, some of which can usually be seen tied up by the village, beside a grassy bank with seats. St Botolph's church is mainly in the Early English style, but with a twentieth-century tower. It is down a side street on the periphery of the modern village. Dedications to St Botolph are usually associated with boundaries, in this case that between Kesteven and Lindsey.

Scawby

This attractive village is situated on the B1207 to the east of Scunthorpe. Its church is dedicated to St Hibald, who gave his name to the neighbouring village of Hibaldstow, where he built a cell in the eighth century, after retiring as Abbot of Bardney. Apart from its medieval west tower, Scawby church was rebuilt in two stages, in 1843 and 1870, and contains monuments to the Nelthorpe family of the adjacent Jacobean Scawby Hall, which can be glimpsed from the unmetalled lane to the north of the church. On the other side of the churchyard and road is a long barn with a pantiled roof where John Wesley is said to have preached. There is a rare cast-iron former Lindsey County Council signpost in the centre of the village, which is a pleasing mixture of stone and brick buildings set amongst trees.

Scopwick

Situated at the crossroads of the B1188 and the B1191, Scopwick (the name means 'sheep farm') stands amongst trees on both banks of a brook. Although largely rebuilt in 1852 and 1884, Holy Cross church retains some medieval work. It contains an effigy of a cross-legged knight. To the east along the B1191, in the hamlet of Kirkby Green, is one of the last remaining fords in the area. Two watermills also survive in this hamlet.

Scotter

There are six place names in Lincolnshire and South Humberside with the prefix 'Scot', referring to the Irish (the Scots having originally come from Ulster to settle amongst the Celts in Strathclyde). Scotter was formerly a small market town on a cross-county road that led to a ferry across the Trent near Susworth. Now the High Street runs at right angles to the main traffic route, the A159 Scunthorpe to Gainsborough road. Situated on the banks of the river Eau, a tributary of the Trent, it has a small but pleasant green looking down to the bridge, with the handsome Georgian manor house on the opposite bank. A pleasant riverside walk has been laid out amongst flowering cherry trees. The horse and pleasure fairs, granted by a charter of Richard I in the twelfth century, and the Thursday market have gone, but Scotter is still a bustling place. The Norman church of St Peter on its southern outskirts contains monuments to the powerful Tyrwhit family, including the brass to Marmaduke, his wife and their ten children.

Scredington

Scredington packhorse bridge, page 69.

Scunthorpe

Early closing Thursday: market days Monday, Friday and Saturday.

Originally a churchless hamlet of Frodingham, Scunthorpe developed during the second half of the nineteenth century under the influence of Rowland Winn (first Baron St Oswald), who began to extract iron ore from his Low Santon estate in 1860. It was on 20th January 1864 that the first steel furnace was fired in Scunthorpe. Amongst other benefactions to the growing town, Winn gave the money to build the church of St John in 1891. He entered Parliament and became successively Conservative Chief Whip and Disraeli's Treasury minister (1874-80). The old Early English St Lawrence's church, Frodingham (near the railway station), was expanded in 1913, so that the former nave became the south aisle, leaving the tower to one side of the enlarged building. Along the A159 are two interesting modern churches in the suburb of Brumby: the Anglican St Hugh's (1939) and the Methodist St Mark's (1960). Along Ashby High Street is the unfinished St Paul's parish church (1925) and its accompanying church hall (1939), beside the polished red granite war memorial. Scunthorpe's own war memorial outside the museum is also worth admiring. In the 1970s a large shopping precinct was built at the rear of the bus station in striking red brick, with a futuristic openwork clock-tower.

Normanby Hall and Country Park, page 92; **Normanby Hall Farming Museum**, page 93; **Scunthorpe Borough Museum and Art Gallery**, page 99.

In the locality: Elsham Hall Country and Wildlife Park, page 60.

Sempringham

Church of St Andrew, page 80.

Sibsey

Lade Bank Pumping Station, page 104; Trader Mill, page 106.

Silk Willoughby

Originally two separate communities of Silkby and Willoughby, they have been joined as one under the present unusual name for centuries. The village was bypassed in 1993 when the A15 was taken along the new Sleaford West relief road. Visitors can now

The 'Jolly Fisherman' statue in the Clock Tower Gardens at Skegness.

better enjoy the parish church of St Denis (a popular dedication in the Sleaford area). Opposite is the base of the village cross on which are carved the symbols of the four evangelists.

Skegness

Early closing Thursday.

Skegness was a port in Tudor times, but the great North Sea surge of 1571 swept much of it away. St Clement's church (dedicated to a patron saint of sailors) was marooned inland. The present seaside resort was planned by the principal landowner, the Earl of Scarbrough.

With the arrival of the railway in 1873 the influx of workers and their families from the Midlands began. Costing £20,000, Skegness pier was opened on 4th June 1881. At 1843 feet (562 metres) it was the fourth longest in Britain. It survived many threats to its existence but finally succumbed to a North Sea gale on the night of 11th January 1978. The Lumley Hotel of 1883 opposite the railway station and James Fowler's impressive St Matthew's church of 1880 were also built to cater for the holidaymakers.

Along the seafront the Jubilee Clock Tower of 1899 has been joined by the new Embassy Centre of 1983 as part of the holiday scene, made famous by the Jolly Fisherman poster of 1908 and the slogan 'Skegness is so bracing!' In 1936 Sir Billy Butlin opened his first holiday camp to the north of the town, now called Funcoast World, with a monorail and a chair lift. The lifeboat station with the *Charles Fred Grantham* is the last remaining one along this coast, and the boat has to be towed into the water by a caterpillar tractor when needed.

Church Farm Museum, page 99; **Natureland Sea Sanctuary**, page 111.

In the locality: Gibraltar Point National Nature Reserve, page 62; Hardy's Animal Farm, page 110.

Skendleby

Down a lane that links the A1028 and the A158 on the foothills of the Wolds, Arthur Mee's description of Skendleby as 'a charming village' is most apt. Its comparatively long main street is on the left bank of a stream that is a tributary of the river Lymm. Its little low-roofed public house, its early nineteenth-century post office, old Victorian school and cobbled side street all form a backcloth to the parish church of St Peter and St Paul, restored by Sir George Gilbert Scott in 1876-8 and containing a fine Kempe stained glass window of 1908, depicting St Hugh (with Lincoln Cathedral) and St Botolph (with Boston Stump).

Skillington

On the borders of Leicestershire to the southwest of Grantham is the well-built village of Skillington. St James's church has Anglo-Saxon long and short work in its nave but its chief interest is its links with two famous Englishmen. The first was Sir Isaac Newton, who is said to have begun his education in a small school held in the transept. The second was the Reverend Charles Hudson, who was vicar from 1859 until his tragic death on 14th July 1865 while descending the Matterhorn after Edward Whymper's renowned first climb of the Alpine peak. There are various mementoes of this event in the church. The fine village green leads up to the sturdy Methodist church of 1847.

Sleaford

Early closing Thursday; market day Monday.

Until April 1974 Sleaford was the county town of Parts of Kesteven. It is situated on the river Slea on the edge of the Fens. This river was turned into the Slea Navigation in 1794 and operated as such until 1881. In Sleaford a new cut formed a small island, which acted as a roundabout for boats terminating in the town centre.

St Denys's church has one of the oldest stone spires in Britain, reaching a height of 144 feet (44 metres). According to Sir Nikolaus Pevsner, it has some of the best examples of flowing window tracery in England, dating from *c.*1360 to 1430. It contains several of the Carre (or Carr) family monuments. They were responsible for Carre's Grammar School (1604) and Carre's Hospital.

In Money's Yard, off Carre Street, the sailless tower windmill, Money's Mill, stands in the middle of a new shopping precinct and houses the tourist information centre.

Down Southgate is the Black Bull inn of 1689 and the canopied statue of Henry Handley, who was member of Parliament for South Lincolnshire from 1832 until 1841.

On the southern fringe of the town are the remarkable maltings of 1905, which consist of eight detached pavilions, with a total frontage of almost 1000 feet (305 metres). This unique industrial complex was badly damaged by a fire, which gutted the central section in the 1970s.

Cogglesford Watermill, page 102; **Maltings**, page 106.

In the locality: Ancaster Valley, page 61; Scredington packhorse bridge, page 69; Cranwell Aviation Heritage Centre, page 94; North Ings Farm Museum, page 95.

Sloothby
Carpenter's shop, page 106.

Snarford
Church of St Lawrence, page 80.

Somersby
Stockwith Mill, page 107.

South Kyme
South Kyme Priory, page 70.

South Somercotes
Church of St Peter, page 80.

South Willingham
Almost within sight of the towering Belmont television mast, at 1250 feet (379 metres) tall Britain's highest man-made structure, thatched cottages nestle against St Michael's church by a sunken lane. The church is built of local greenstone and has a Perpendicular-style tower, although the chancel was rebuilt in 1779 and the nave in 1838.

South Witham
Geeson Bros Motorcycle Museum, page 99.

Spalding
Early closing Thursday; market days Tuesday and Saturday.

The heart of Tulipland, Spalding receives half a million visitors on the occasion of the annual Tulip Parade at the beginning of May each year. Those who miss the Saturday's parade can view the decorated floats at Springfields, the 22 acre (8.9 hectare) site on the A151 Holbeach road, opened in April 1966 in the Fulney suburb of Spalding. Behind Springfields tower four 198 feet (60 metres) high sugar-beet silos, each capable of holding 12,000 tons. The factory was opened by the Anglo-Scottish Sugar Beet Company in 1926.

There are few relics of Spalding's Benedictine priory, founded in about 1087 as a cell

St Denys's church in the centre of Sleaford.

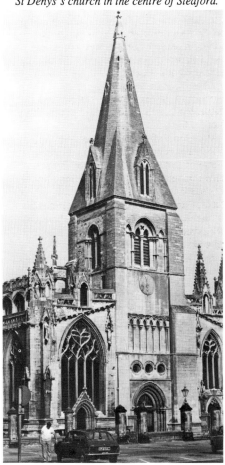

Stamford is a busy shopping centre as well as an elegant Georgian town.

The village lake in the centre of Tathwell, near Louth.

The war memorial in the grounds of Ayscoughfee Hall, Spalding.

of St Nicholas's, Angers, by Thorold of Buckendale, the brother of Lady Godiva. Just off Priory Road are some old almshouses that may have been part of the priory's domestic buildings. The same is claimed for the Prior's Oven café in the Sheep Market. Round the corner in the Market Place stands the White Hart coaching inn, built about 1714 and, although badly bombed during the Second World War, well restored. A hostelry has stood on this spot from at least 1377.

Along the banks of the river Welland are many fine town houses, including Welland Terrace of 1813, looking across to Ayscoughfee (pronounced 'Asscuffy') Hall, built originally by Sir Richard Aldwyn in 1429; some of the original building survives, such as the tower. It was the home of Maurice Johnson (1688-1755), founder in 1710 of the Gentlemen's Society of Spalding, which is still flourishing at its Broad Street headquarters. Nowadays Ayscoughfee Hall contains the society's collection of stuffed birds. In the grounds is a fine war memorial looking down to an ornamental pond that once provided blocks of ice for the surviving icehouse, tucked in one corner of the garden walls. At the rear of the hall is the parish church of Saints Mary and Nicholas (the latter a re-

minder that Spalding was once an inland port) of *c*.1284, with fourteenth- and fifteenth-century additions. The spire reaches a height of 160 feet (49 metres). Its hammerbeam roof is decorated with twenty-eight carved wooden angels.

Ayscoughfee Hall and Gardens, page 99; **Pinchbeck Engine**, page 105; **Pode Hole Pumping Station**, page 106; **railway footbridges**, page 107; **Springfields Gardens**, page 111; **Tulip Parade**, page 121.

In the locality: Museum of Entertainment, page 100.

Spilsby

Early closing Tuesday; market day Monday.
This is the smallest surviving market town in Lincolnshire and is situated near the southern extremity of the Wolds. It originated as a crossroads hamlet to the larger village of Eresby, the home of the Willoughby family, ennobled by Edward II in 1313, and whose seat is Grimsthorpe Castle, near Bourne. Only a few cottages, the former stables of Eresby Hall and a single gatepost are left at Eresby, which was devastated by fire in 1749. The family monuments up to the reign of James I are in a side chapel of St James's church in Spilsby.

In the Market Place stand the statue of Sir John Franklin, the explorer who lost his life in 1847 while searching for the North-west Passage and who was born in the town, and the former town hall of 1764. At the other end of the Market Place (the centre having been infilled with shops) is the medieval market cross, which may be fourteenth-century. In the opposite direction is the stately Sessions House of 1826; quarter sessions for Lindsey were held here until 1878, and since 1984 it has been the home of the Spilsby Theatre. Almost opposite this stretches Eresby Avenue, a picturesque avenue of trees with the solitary Eresby Hall gatepost visible at its far end.

In the locality: Bolingbroke Castle, page 68; Gunby Hall, page 90; Fenside Goat Centre, page 110.

Stainton-le-Vale

Formerly called Stainton-in-the-Hole, this secluded hamlet on the Waithe Beck is tucked in the northern part of the Wolds near the busy village of Binbrook. It is reached down a steep, narrow lane off High Street (the prehistoric ridgeway that runs between Caistor and Horncastle). The tiny St Andrew's parish church retains its Norman nave, which has been charmingly painted in two shades of pink. There is a restored painting of the Italian school hanging there in memory of a local schoolgirl who died in 1971. On a sunny day the hamlet is a delightful sight.

Stamford

Early closing Thursday; market day Friday.
Of all the towns of Lincolnshire perhaps the most pleasing is Stamford with its cream-coloured stone buildings and medieval churches grouped round the town centre. It is a good idea to view the town from the A1 bypass before beginning to explore its narrow streets and lanes.

Although there were once twice as many churches in the town centre, within its medieval stone walls, as there are today, those that have survived are all worth visiting. The two with spires are All Saints' and St Mary's. The former has been described by Sir Nikolaus Pevsner as 'the hub of Stamford'. Its most famous incumbent was Dr William Stukeley in the early eighteenth century. It has some interesting blank arcading along its exterior walls. Inside are brasses to the Browne family, who became rich in the late middle ages on the wool trade (hence William Browne, founder of Browne's Hospital, is shown standing on two woolsacks). St Mary's is a fine Early English style church in a prominent position on the former Great North Road looking down towards the river Welland. In its north chapel is an excellent stone figure of a lady c.1330. There are also the effigies of Sir David Phillips and his wife (1506). Behind St Mary's is St George's, rebuilt after the Lancastrian sack of the town in 1461. It is chiefly renowned for its stained glass, which includes two figures of the mid fifteenth century and about two hundred mottoes of the early members of the Order of the Garter, assembled in 1732. On the corner of High Street stands St John the Baptist's, a plain Perpendicular-style building, but again with late medieval glass and brasses. Further up High Street is St Michael's, completely rebuilt in 1836 and now converted into shops. Medieval St Paul's church has become the chapel of Stamford School.

On the other side of the river, in the suburb known as either Stamford Baron or St Martin's Without, is the church of that name, largely rebuilt about 1480 and containing the fine tomb of William Cecil, first Lord Burghley. In the burial ground down a footpath beside the church is the massive grave of Daniel Lambert, the famous fat man, who died in the town while visiting the races in 1809.

Browne's Hospital is in Broad Street. Its chapel was consecrated in 1494, five years after the death of the benefactor. Much of the hospital was rebuilt in 1870. In Broad Street cattle markets were held until the late nineteenth century and each November from 1209 until 1839 the local sport of bull running took place. Down by the bridge is another long-established hospital, Burghley's, founded in 1597 on the site of the former medieval one dedicated to St John the Baptist and St Thomas the Martyr (Becket). This was refurbished in 1849.

St Mary's church, Stamford, viewed through the gallows sign of the George of Stamford Hotel.

There are a few remains of medieval houses along St Mary's Hill. Number 13 dates from about 1220, whilst number 11 may be as old as *c*.1150. Down West Street there is the last remaining bastion of the town walls.

Georgian Stamford is represented by some fine buildings. Apart from the famous George Hotel (rebuilt at the end of the eighteenth century), the Town Hall (1777) and the Assembly Rooms in St George's Square (1725), there is the 1809 Stamford Hotel with Rossi's statue of Justice surmounting it. This has been converted into eighteen small shops.

It was the remarkable completeness of Stamford's Georgian architecture that attracted the BBC when it was looking for a location in which to film George Eliot's *Middlemarch*. St George's Square, St Mary's Street, Barn Hill and All Saints Place were all used to re-create street scenes of the 1830s.

Little can be seen of the friaries and other monastic houses of Stamford, apart from the gateway to Whitefriars in St Paul's Street and part of St Leonard's Priory.

The grave of Sir Malcolm Sargent, the conductor, who died in 1967, is in the town's cemetery along Casterton Road. On his simple marble cross is inscribed the Promenaders' Prayer.

Burghley Park and House lie to the east of the town.

In 1971 the amateur Stamford Shakespeare Company was established to present a summer season of plays at the George inn. However, in 1976, the company moved out of the town to Tolethorpe Hall (just off the A6121 Bourne road at TF 023102). Here open-air performances are given for six weeks each summer.

St Leonard's Priory, page 71; **Burghley House**, page 82; **Stamford Museum**, page 100; **Stamford Brewery Museum**, page 100; **Museum of Almshouse Life**, page 100; **Stamford East railway station**, page 107; **Tallington Lakes**, page 111.

Stickford

Now bypassed by the A16, Stickford is the most northerly of the three villages that lay astride the narrow causeway that links Boston with the Wolds, and divided the erstwhile East and West Fens (drained by steam pumps in the early nineteenth century). The village possesses a splendid war memorial clock

The river Nene at Sutton Bridge.

tower. Although much of St Helen's church was either restored or rebuilt in the nineteenth century, the Perpendicular-style greenstone tower is worth examining, as it has a blocked-up processional way through the tower at ground level. A barn on the opposite side of the former A16 retains a yellow and black AA village sign, which becomes obscured by creeper during the summer months!
Allied Forces Military Museum, page 100.

Stoke Rochford

In the 1840s the Turnor family had North Stoke village with its St Andrew's church demolished in order to impark in connection with the building of the new Stoke Rochford Hall. South Stoke's St Mary's church was partly rebuilt and given its present double dedication. At the same time the village was rebuilt with stone estate cottages and renamed Stoke Rochford. The church contains the memorials of the ancient Rochford family, as well as those of the Cholmeley (pronounced 'Chumly') family of Easton Hall on the opposite side of the A1. In the grounds of the hall (now the National Union of Teachers Conference Centre) there is a 60 feet (18 metres) high obelisk erected in 1847 in hon-

our of Sir Isaac Newton, who is said to have attended a dame school in the village.

Stow

Church of St Mary, page 80.

Stragglethorpe

Down a lane on the south side of the A17 trunk road between Leadenham and Newark lies the hamlet of Stragglethorpe, famous for its vineyards, attached to Stragglethorpe Hall. Although the hall was originally erected in Elizabethan times on an H plan, it has been added to and altered over the intervening centuries. The little church of St Michael has a medieval appearance, and its west wall dates from Anglo-Saxon times. The low ceiling emphasises its antiquity. There is an interesting funeral oration on the monument of Sir Richard Earle, Baronet, of 1697.
In the locality: Brant Broughton church, page 74.

Sutton Bridge

Once a railway junction and would-be port, Sutton Bridge is nowadays chiefly remembered as a traffic bottleneck on the busy A17, where cars and lorries cross the river Nene on the swing bridge of 1897, to enter Norfolk along a huge embankment over the fen. This was completed in 1831 and its construction had occupied 900 men and 260 horses for five years. A further 1500 labourers had excavated a new tideway for the river. This leads out to the two Guy's Head lighthouses, one of which was once the home of Sir Peter Scott, when he began to study wildfowl. Near this is King John's Farm, traditionally one of the sites where that monarch's treasure convoy was said to have been overtaken by the swiftly moving tide of the Wash in 1216.

In the very long village, St Matthew's parish church of 1843 in knapped flint with stone dressings is more reminiscent of Norfolk than of Lincolnshire. The High Street contains some handsome terraces, such as numbers 44, 46 and 48, whilst the Bridge Hotel and nearby warehousing remind the visitor of the attempt to create a dock here in 1881. This collapsed into the river after only a month but new wharfs were opened in 1986.

Sutton-on-Sea
Early closing Thursday.
Although linked to Mablethorpe by local government and by a ribbon of caravans and holiday camps along the tortuous A52, the character of Sutton-on-Sea is different from that of its neighbour. For four years steam trams from Alford terminated outside the Jolly Bacchus hotel near the seafront. Eleven people lost their lives during the North Sea flood of 31st January 1953 (compared with eight at Mablethorpe), and most of the population were evacuated to Louth, while troops and workmen poured 25,000 tons of slag into the gaps in the sea defences. The Canadian people presented Sutton residents with the Maple Leaf paddling pool as a gift afterwards.

At very low tides parts of a 7500-year-old submerged forest can be seen here and at Huttoft Bank several miles further south.

The place was once called Sutton-in-the-Marsh and the aptness of that earlier title becomes apparent as you travel past the 1818 red brick St Clement's church on the way to Skegness.

In the locality: Claythorpe Watermill and Wildfowl Gardens, page 109.

Sutton St James
St Ives Cross, page 71.

Swineshead
In Shakespeare's *King John* (act V, scene VII) that unhappy monarch is resting in the orchard of 'Swinstead Abbey'. In fact, on 12th October 1216 John was staying for a few hours at the Cistercian abbey of Swineshead, situated down a lane in the satellite hamlet of Barthorpe. The village's name has nothing to do with pigs, but with the river Swin (long disappeared due to modern drainage).

Until the seventeenth century Swineshead was a small market town. It still retains a fourteenth-century cross base, with the war memorial and garden.

Tathwell
The dedication of its parish church to St Vedast is unique. He was a bishop of Arras, who died in 539, and is chiefly remembered for saving the life of a goose grabbed by a fox – a story which is depicted in a 1923 memorial window. In recent years local people have raised money to restore the 1626 wall monument to Edward Hanby, the sentiments of which are quite touching. In the churchyard stands the red marble Tuscan Doric column in memory of Lord William Henry Cavendish Bentinck, son of a Duke of Portland. The village nestles in a hollow in the Wolds near Louth and is graced by a lake and a flowing stream beside the main street. Nearby are Bully Hills (see page 65).

Tattershall
Tattershall Castle Country Club, page 111; Tattershall Castle, page 71; church of Holy Trinity, page 80.

Tattershall Bridge
Dogdyke Steam Pumping Station, page 103; 'Tales of the River Bank' visitor centre, page 107.

Tealby
Bayons Manor, the eccentric fairyland castle created by Charles Tennyson d'Eyncourt and the architect W. A. Nicholson in the late 1830s, was blown up as a dangerous ruin

about 1970, but there are still reminders of Lord Tennyson's uncle in All Saints' church, high above Tealby village. Members of the family lie in a vault under the 1872 chancel. However, much of this ironstone church dates from medieval and Norman times.

The charm of Tealby is its grid of narrow streets of individual cottages with their colourful gardens: Cow Lane, Beck Hill, Front Street, Sandy Lane. The diminutive river Rase flows across a ford near a watermill, and down amongst the water meadows is the thatched King's Head public house.

Tetford

This fair-sized village lies in the heart of the Wolds to the south of Louth at the foot of the ridgeway that carries the Bluestone Heath prehistoric road. It is built round four sides of a large square of enclosed fields, with the greenstone parish church of St Mary at one corner and the Methodist chapel diagonally opposite it. The White Hart inn is said to date from about 1520 and in 1764 Dr Samuel Johnson (who often visited nearby Gunby Hall) addressed the Tetford Club here. The Roman road from Lincoln to Burgh-le-Marsh forms the line of the northern side of the square, beyond which is the hamlet of Little London (a popular name for such an adjacent

settlement in Lincolnshire). Tetford's national school of 1822, although now a private house, served the village until the late 1970s.

In the locality: Stockwith Mill, page 107.

Theddlethorpe

Nowadays the village's name is associated with the nearby Conoco North Sea Gas Terminal, which was opened in 1972. There are two communities: Theddlethorpe St Helens and Theddlethorpe All Saints. The medieval church of the latter was restored after being closed and, as a fine example of a marshland church, has been placed under the aegis of the Redundant Churches Fund. This part of the village also contains the former railway stationmaster's house on the disused line from Louth to Mablethorpe, and further down the settlement's long village street is the thatched mud and stud King's Head inn. Along the busy A1031 lies St Helen's church with its greenstone tower in the Perpendicular style, rebuilt by the architect S. S. Teulon in 1864-7. Just beyond the parish boundary lies the Gayton Engine House, recently restored.

Gayton Engine, page 103.

Threekingham

Although the public house of the Three Kings claims to be connected with the burial of

Tealby owes its charm to its narrow streets and picturesque cottages.

The ruined Elizabethan manor overlooking the river Trent at Torksey.

three Danish kings following a bloody battle at nearby Stow Green, there appears to be no justification for this link. Threekingham (pronounced Threckingham) is now bypassed by the A52, and the visitor can wander around the village and enjoy the Norman chancel of St Peter's church (one of the very few dedications to be listed in Domesday for the county). This is located near the crossroads where the ancient Salter's Way went from east to west for the packhorse delivery of sea salt, and Mareham Lane going north to south was used not only by the Romans but also by merchants, pedlars and others travelling to and from the great medieval fair at Stow Green. Near this crossroads stands the last survivor of a number of whalebone arches which were erected in this part of Kesteven.

Torksey

Listed as one of the very few towns in Lincolnshire in the Domesday Book (1086), it is situated near the junction of the river Trent and the Roman Fossdyke canal on the A156 to the south of Gainsborough. In the middle ages it had a house of Augustinian canons (founded before 1216, with a church dedicated to St Leonard), Fosse Priory for Cistercian nuns (founded about 1218, with a church dedicated to St Nicholas), three parish churches (All Saints', St Mary's and St Peter's) and a castle. Of all these only St Peter's survives with its Perpendicular tower and Early English nave.

The present so-called 'castle' is the ruin of Robert Jermyn's mansion on the banks of the Trent and dating from the end of the reign of Elizabeth I. It had a short life, being burnt down during a skirmish here on 1st August 1645. It had been taken by the Parliamentarians the previous September, but a raiding party from the Royalist garrison at Newark Castle destroyed it the following summer. In an attempt to prevent such a foray Cromwell's troops had flooded much of the Torksey area, causing over £500 worth of damage.

In the locality: churches at Marton, page 79, and Stow, page 80.

Toynton All Saints

Fenside Goat Centre, page 110.

A delightful estate cottage in the village of Uffington.

Uffington

Situated on the A16 between Market Deeping and Stamford, this village is built in the delightful cream stone quarried from nearby Barnack and with roof 'slates' from Collyweston to the south of Stamford. The parish church of St Michael has a fine Perpendicular tower with a recessed crocketed spire and probably dates from about 1490. There is a good collection of monuments inside, for the village contained two mansions. Uffington House, the seat of the Earls of Lindsey, and dating from about 1681, was burnt down in 1904. However, John Lumley's ornamental garden gates of *c.*1700 opposite the church remain, as does the Georgian lodge at the Market Deeping end of the village. The other great house is Casewick Hall, just over a mile down the side road near the church. In 1621 this became the home of William Trollop of Thurlby-near-Bourne, who began its rebuilding. It stands in a large park. Back in the village is the charming thatched Bertie Arms (the family name of the Earls of Lindsey).

Utterby

Utterby packhorse bridge, page 73.

Wainfleet

Early closing Thursday; market day Saturday.

The large parish of Wainfleet, situated along the banks of the Steeping River near its entry into the Wash, was once divided into the three ecclesiastical divisions of All Saints, St Mary and St Thomas (of Canterbury). All Saints grew into a small port and market town. St Thomas has become the suburb of Northolme in All Saints parish. St Mary remains a small and isolated marshland village.

All Saints' church itself was rebuilt in stock brick in 1821 and is disappointing to look at. Much more interesting is Magdalen School, built of dark red brick by Henry Alsbroke in 1484 for its founder William of Waynflete (*c.* 1395-1486), born locally, Lord Chancellor to Henry VI and Bishop of Winchester from 1447 until his death.

In the rough Market Place stands a medieval knob cross and the clock-tower of 1899. At the back of it, closed to vehicular traffic, is the handsome Barkham Street of High Victorian date.

In the locality: Gibraltar Point National Nature Reserve, page 62.

Waltham

The centre of this commuter village on the south-western periphery of Grimsby is a delightful green on which there is an anvil, a memorial to Henry Jackson, the village's last blacksmith. All Saints' church has the very old in the reused Roman stone in its nave and chancel, as well as the very new in a modern annexe that links it with the church hall. From the period in between, there is the brass to Joanna Waltham (died 1420) and her children. Half a mile (800 metres) down the B1203 to the south of Waltham is the six-sailed mill with accompanying craft centre and extensive miniature railway layout.

Tower mill, page 107.

Welbourn

The half-cucumber shape of the Decorated-period crocketed spire that surmounts the tower of St Chad's parish church looks very distinctive and striking from the A607 Lincoln to Grantham road, which bypasses the village. The whole church is very handsome and owes much to the generosity of John of Welbourn, Treasurer of Lincoln Cathedral, who died in 1380. However, the church contains a memorial tablet to a more famous local man, Field Marshal Sir William Robertson, Baronet, who was born in a small house at the other end of the village (the one with a shop front in a terrace) in 1860. He joined the British Army as a private seventeen years later and, after seeing service in India and in the Second Boer War, became a staff officer, ending his brilliant career as Commander-in-Chief of the British Army on the Rhine in 1919. He died in 1933, the first man ever to serve in all the ranks in the British army.

Castle Hill, near the church, consists of a circular earthwork, which is known to have had stone walls in the mid twelfth century. The Manor House of the seventeenth century is one of several fine buildings in this attractive village.

In the locality. Temple Bruer, page 72.

Wellingore

The unusual name of this village has nothing to do with blood, but everything to do with

people by a stream on an edge – in this case Lincoln Cliff. The Ordnance Survey bench-mark by the church proclaims it to be at 245 feet (74 metres) above mean sea level, and the land drops away steeply from All Saints' churchyard, with its marvellous views across the Brant and Witham valley and across to the spire of neighbouring Welbourn church. At the other end of this village astride the A607 stands a medieval cross where the modern Lincoln to Grantham road deviated from the line of Roman Ermine Street. The village's 1854 windmill tower still stands, although now converted into a residence. Search out Wellingore Hall (*c.*1750), the Manor House (Georgian) and The Cottage (1670), as well as Greystone which epitomises this Kesteven settlement.

In the locality: Somerton Castle, page 69.

Westborough

Lying on the right bank of the river Witham downstream from Grantham and roughly op-

William of Waynflete, Lord Chancellor to Henry VI, built Magdalen School in his native town of Wainfleet.

posite Long Bennington (on the A1), Westborough has become popular as a commuter village. It has a large triangular green dominated by a flagpole and with a five-stepped medieval cross. All Saints' church is so near the river that it suffers perpetually from dampness, but it is a light and historic building, with a twelfth-century nave and an Early English wide chancel, divided from the nave by curtains. In 1750 part of the church collapsed and in its rebuilding a domestic-looking five-light window was inserted. At the same time the tower was rebuilt. The churchyard has some bold black modern gates. Behind the high brick wall to the north of All Saints is the imposing rectory with an eighteenth-century façade and a seventeenth-century rear.

West Rasen

West Rasen packhorse bridge, page 73.

Whaplode St Catherine

Museum of Entertainment, page 100.

Winceby

Snipe Dales Country Park, page 60.

Winteringham

Near the present village the Romans had a ferry crossing of the Humber to their posting station of *Petuaria* (Brough-on-Humber), from where travellers could continue their journey along Ermine Street to York and beyond. The waters of the river can be very rough, and in 1641 the ferry capsized, drowning the father of the poet Andrew Marvell.

The church of All Saints has served the former port and town since Norman times and contains the effigy of a thirteenth-century cross-legged knight.

Winterton

This ancient town has received a new lease of life since the Second World War and its population is almost 5000. Lying between the A1077 (Scunthorpe to Barton-upon-Humber road) and the B1207 (Ermine Street), it stands just to the north of the iron ore belt which has brought prosperity to the area in the twentieth century. The Romans had an extensive villa

complex on the steep slopes of Winterton Beck to the west of the town, and this was partly excavated in the early nineteenth century by a local architect, William Fowler, whose house, The Chains, was designed by himself and still stands as number 35 West Street. He drew detailed plans of the mosaic floors before the site was infilled. More thorough excavations took place in the 1970s.

There are two contrasting churches in Winterton. All Saints' church has an Anglo-Saxon tower, whilst Trinity Methodist church has a four-legged openwork tower that peers over the surrounding roof tops. There are some interesting houses in Park Street, including the Old Hall dating from the mid seventeenth century.

Woodhall Spa

Early closing Wednesday.

While sinking a trial shaft for coal in 1821 John Parkinson discovered instead a supply of water, which Thomas Hotchkin had analysed thirteen years later. It contained both iodine and bromine. As a result Hotchkin built a small bath-house in 1834 and from that date the spa began to grow on a 60 acre (24 hectare) site, set in sandy woodlands more reminiscent of Surrey than of Lincolnshire. The buildings included the Victoria Hotel (1839), the Alexandra Hospital (1890) and the Royal Hydro (1897). At the last, hypertonic saline waters were heated to 103°F (40°C). The arrival of the Horncastle branch of the Great Northern Railway in 1855 made Woodhall Spa easily accessible. The spa pumping house collapsed into the well in 1983.

The original parish church of St Andrew, situated at the crossroads in the centre of the town, was built in 1850 but has since been demolished. Opposite is the new Dambusters Memorial.

St Peter's was designed by Charles Hodgson Fowler in 1893 and has its counterpart in the Methodist church on the other side of the B1191 spine road. On the northern outskirts of the town is a fragment of the hunting lodge constructed for Lord Ralph Cromwell of Tattershall Castle in the mid fifteenth century. It is locally referred to as the Tower-on-the-Moor and stands adjacent to the golf course.

The Dambusters Memorial in Royal Square is a tribute to 617 Squadron in the form of a model breeched dam 20 feet (6 metres) long. The officers' mess of this unit was situated nearby at the Petwood Hotel, which has a Squadron Bar full of memorabilia of 617.

Other attractions at Woodhall Spa include the unusual Kinema-in-the-Woods, Jubilee Park and the Wellington Monument by Waterloo Wood in the neighbouring hamlet of Reed's Beck. This was erected in 1844 to celebrate the successful cultivation of an oak wood sown with acorns in June 1815.

Cottage Museum, page 100.

In the locality: Kirkstead Abbey, page 68; Tupholme Abbey, page 73. See also Coningsby, Tattershall and Tattershall Bridge.

Woolsthorpe-by-Belvoir

Tucked in at the foot of the opposite hill to that on which the Duke of Rutland's Belvoir Castle (pronounced 'Beaver') stands is this attractive little village which is on the borders of Lincolnshire and Leicestershire. St James's parish church is of ironstone (much of which has been quarried in the area in the twentieth century) and was rebuilt in 1847 in the traditional Decorated style. In a similar style is the 1871 village school. Down on the banks of the disused Grantham to Nottingham Canal is a hamlet from where stone and coal were hauled up to Belvoir Castle.

In the locality: Harlaxton Manor and Gardens, page 91.

Wootton

Within sight of the Killingholme oil refineries lies this quiet little village, where the main street meets the A1077 to Barrow-upon-Humber by a delightful pond, with its notice warning drivers to beware of ducks! The little ironstone church of St Andrew is worth looking at, as is Wootton Hall (seventeenth century) and the Old Vicarage (mainly Georgian), which at one time had a Victorian folly in its grounds, erected to hide a pigsty.

Wragby

This former small market town lies on a cross-roads where the main A158 (Lincoln to Skegness road) meets the A157 from Louth and the B1202 (Market Rasen to Bardney). Along the Skegness road are All Saints' church of 1838 and the old railway station on the former single-track line that joined Louth with Bardney from 1876 until 1951. The remains of the former parish church lie just to the south of All Saints' and consist merely of a brick chancel.

Away from the large triangular Market Place, along the A157 are the new town hall and a modern works manufacturing beehives and beekeeping equipment.

In the locality: Barlings Abbey, page 68; Langworth Animal Park, page 111.

Wrangle

This is one of these widely dispersed villages that lie astride the A52 between Wainfleet and Boston. Fortunately the village centre has been bypassed and is a quiet spot, where is located St Nicholas's church and the war memorial. Inside the former are two interesting brasses, depicting John Reade (died 1503) and Sir John Reade (died 1626). The churchyard cross was converted into a sundial in 1826. Wrangle in the middle ages stood on an inlet of the Wash and had connections with the Staple of Calais, but in the intervening centuries the land between the village and the sea has been reclaimed for agricultural purposes.

Wrawby

Wrawby Post Mill, page 108.

3
The countryside

Elsham Hall Country and Wildlife Park, Brigg, South Humberside DN20 0QZ (OS 112: TA 030120). Telephone: 01652 688698. By the junction of B1204 and B1218 (former A15) north-east of Brigg.

Open: Easter to mid-September, daily; rest of the year, Sundays only.

Basically an eighteenth-century mansion, Elsham Hall is the home of the Elwes family. The grounds have been laid out as a country park, with falconry, conservation centre, carp-feeding jetty, wild butterfly garden, arboretum and children's animal farm. There are craft workshops, the Barn Theatre, a restaurant and tearooms.

Hubbard's Hills, Louth (OS 122: TF 318870). At the west end of Louth, ap-proached via Crowtree Lane.

This area is not really hills at all, but a narrow valley with precipitous sides, formed by glacial meltwaters 40,000 years ago. The small river Lud now flows through it, normally shallow enough to allow small children to paddle in it. The name derives from Alexander Hubbard, a local farmer, who died in the nearby hamlet of Hallington in 1793. This little valley was purchased for the town of Louth under the terms of the will of Auguste Alphonse Pahud, a Swiss immigrant schoolmaster, who committed suicide in 1902. The fountain temple beside the Lud contains a commemorative plaque to him.

There is a band of exposed pink chalk at the town end of the valley. The Lud widens into a small pond near there and is the haunt of

The grounds of eighteenth-century Elsham Hall, near Brigg, are now a country and wildlife park.

mallard and moorhen. A café serves ices and light refreshments at peak holiday times.

Snipe Dales Country Park, Winceby, Horncastle (OS 122: TF 330682). Telephone: 01507 588401. North of the B1195 Horncastle to Spilsby road, at Winceby.
Open daily.
This is near the site of the battle of Winceby, which took place in October 1643, when the Royalists were routed by Cromwell. Snipe Dales consists of a series of steep-sided valleys in the soft Spilsby sandstone. In the valley bottoms grow ferns and marsh marigolds. meadowsweet, ragged robin and hairy willowherb. Amongst the fauna to be seen are short-eared owl, kestrel, woodcock, heron, snipe and badger. The Lincolnshire Trust for Nature Conservation has managed the site for the county council since 1974, and visitors are requested to follow strictly the marked routes. In 1985 90 acres (36 hectares) of adjoining woodland were added as a country park.

Nature reserves

With the exception of Bourne Wood and Chambers Farm Wood, the reserves listed in this section are administered by the Lincolnshire Trust for Nature Conservation, Banovallum House, Manor House Street, Horncastle LN9 5HF. Telephone: 01507 526667.

Ancaster Valley, Ancaster, near Sleaford (OS 130: SK 984434).
This is a limestone valley running down the hillside into the Ancaster Gap, with a hanger of beech trees, along with limestone grassland containing many scarce flowers such as the bee orchid and the pasque flower. On calm sunny days there are large numbers of butterflies and bumble-bees to be seen. The entrance is off the A153 to the east of the village crossroads and visitors are asked to keep to the public footpath.

Bourne Wood, near Bourne (OS 130: TF 075201). 1 mile (1.6 km) west of the town on A151. Forestry Commission.
This is a 400 acre (160 hectare) mixture of

The steep sides of Hubbard's Hills valley, near Louth.

broadleaf and conifer trees owned by the Forestry Commission since 1926. It is ancient woodland rich in flowers and animals. Interesting features include a coppicing plot, a pond, and sculptures by local artists.

Chambers Farm Wood (OS 121: TF 148738). East of Lincoln, off the B1202 between Wragby and Bardney. Forestry Commission.
The Forestry Commission has laid out three forest walks through a variety of habitats: ancient woodland, conifer plantations, grass rides, ponds and farmland.

Donna Nook Nature Reserve. 6 miles (10 km) of coastline between North Somercotes and Saltfleet Haven, with the main entrances at Stonebridge (OS 113: TF 422998), Howden

The Gibraltar Point field station of the Lincolnshire Trust for Nature Conservation was formerly a coastguard station.

Pullover (off A1031 at TF 449952) and Sea Lane, Saltfleet (TF 456944).

The dunes support wild flowers, including pyramidal orchids. They are also colonised by marram grass and sea buckthorn. During the summer the area is the nesting site for many species, including dunnock, little grebe and meadow pipit, whilst the mudflats attract large numbers of brent geese, knot, dunlin and other species of waders. The sandflats are the site where both common and grey seals pup.

Far Ings, Barton-upon-Humber, South Humberside DN18 5RG (OS 122: TA 021233). Telephone: 01652 634507. Near the Humber Bridge.

The reserve can be reached via Far Ings Lane, off Waterside, Barton, and consists of a series of disused clay pits and reedbeds from which clay has been extracted for generations to produce the local pantiles. As well as the areas of water, which support up to fifty species of birds, the reserve is home to over one hundred species of moth. There is a visitor centre which includes a wildlife gift shop, a schoolroom and toilets (including those for the disabled). The nature reserve is dedicated to the memory of the late Sam Van den Bos, a

local conservationist. There is also the Westfield Lakes Hotel.

Gibraltar Point National Nature Reserve, Gibraltar Point Field Station, Skegness PE24 4SU (OS 122: TF 556581). Telephone: 01754 762677. Continue south along Drummond Road, Skegness, past the golf links.

After 1526 this 'ness' began to replace that at Skegness, washed away by the North Sea surge of that year. In spite of setbacks caused by subsequent surges such as that in January 1953, Gibraltar Point has been gradually enlarged as one set of sand dunes after another has been formed, enclosing saltmarshes behind them. On these grow sea lavender, while the dunes become colonised by sea buckthorn, which bears distinctive orange berries in the autumn. In 1932 the area was made the responsibility of Lindsey County Council, and in 1948 the present guardians (the Lincolnshire Trust for Nature Conservation) took over the care of Gibraltar Point, setting up a bird observatory with a Heligoland trap. The former coastguard station has become the nucleus of the present field station. A visitor centre was added in 1974 and includes a wildlife gift shop.

Members of the public are welcome to park their cars by the centre and walk along the footpath to the beach and around the reserve, following waymarked routes. There are several birdwatching hides. On summer afternoons there are guided tours of the reserve.

Red Hill, Goulceby, near Louth (OS 122: TF 269806).

This small reserve comprises 10 acres (3.8 hectares) of steep chalk escarpment grassland along with an equivalent area of old plateau grassland, including a disused quarry. There is an exposed vein of red chalk, rich in fossil belamnites and brachiopods, facing the lane. Butterflies and moths of several species inhabit the reserve, as do the meadow pipit, common lizard and grass snake. There are two small car parks.

Whisby Nature Park. Telephone: 01522 500676. South-west of Lincoln off the A46 bypass. Entrance in Moor Lane (OS 121: SK 917677).

This extensive area is made up of 51 acres (20.7 hectares) of nature reserve and 145 acres (58.6 hectares) of nature park on either side of the Lincoln to Newark railway line.

At the entrance, there is a small centre for visitors (with toilets, including those for the disabled) and car park. This is also the starting point for a series of walks. In summer great crested grebe, mallard and moorhen nest on the reserve, whilst it is the wintering quarters for teal, tufted duck and wigeon.

Walks

Blankney Barff Walks. The starting points for these are to be found either off the B1189 down a lane signposted Blankney Fen at OS 121: TF 106610, or else in Martin village on the B1191 at TF 121600.

The walks are marked by yellow arrows on green backgrounds and vary in length from 1²/₃ miles (2.7 km) up to the blue route of 5¹/₂ miles (9 km). The Lincolnshire word 'barff' indicates a hill running parallel with low lying land, and all these walks cover both types of terrain. In places they are along the bank of the Roman Car Dyke. Part of the routes are across the former RAF Metheringham airfield.

The River Slea Trail

This is an 8 mile (13 km) walk along well-trodden paths and tracks, although sturdy shoes and long trousers are strongly recommended! It commences in the centre of Sleaford at Turn-Around Cut on the 1794 Slea Navigation, and leaves the town along its banks, passing Cogglesford Mill and Evedon church, until the turning point is reached at the site of Haverholme Priory. An excellent guide book to this trail is published by North Kesteven District Council.

The Viking Way

This long distance footpath was declared open in 1977 and stretches 136 miles (219 km) from the Humber Bridge to Oakham (the historical county town of Rutland). Its first section is over the Wolds on a somewhat meandering course, signposted by directional signs bearing a horned Viking helmet. Amongst other places, it passes Grasby church, where Tennyson's elder brother, Charles, was vicar for almost forty years; Caistor; Nettleton, an ironstone village by ironstone quarries and mines; Normanby-le-Wold, the highest village in Lincolnshire; Walesby, where the old church of All Saints is known as the ramblers' church; Tealby; and so down into Horncastle.

The second section of the Viking Way goes along the bed of the disused single-track railway that joined Horncastle to Woodhall Spa from 1855 until 1954. From Woodhall Spa the Way swings south-west to join the bank of the river Witham at Southrey for a walk into the centre of Lincoln. After climbing on to Lincoln Cliff or Edge the Way follows the line of Ermine Street between Wellingore and Byard's Leap. After aiming in a westerly direction, the Way heads south along Sewstern Lane, the old route along which cattle were driven towards London in medieval times, until it crosses the border into Leicestershire by the hamlet of Wyville.

There is a booklet on sale at public libraries giving full maps and details of the Way.

Viewing points

From the junction of the A1500 (Tillbridge Lane) and the B1398 at the rear of RAF

Scampton (OS 121: SK 956784) there is a panoramic view over the Trent flood plain to the line of power stations along the Nottinghamshire bank of the river.

South of Lincoln, off the A607 near Welbourn (OS 121: SK 976538), beside the Roman Pottergate there is a viewing point from which the village can be espied, along with the dominating spire of St Helen's, Brant Broughton, towards the flood plain of the river Witham at Beckingham, and beyond to the Trent near Newark.

The third special viewing point is situated on top of the Wolds beside the prehistoric ridgeway known as the Bluestone Heath Road (OS 122: TF 317761), and above the village of Tetford. From here the undulating arable land of the Wolds can be admired.

Picnic sites

In most cases there is ample parking space available, along with wooden tables and benches. They are listed approximately in a north to south order.

Barrow-on-Humber (OS 112: TA 053218). Beside the A1077 Barton-upon-Humber road.

From here there is a panoramic view of shipping on the Humber, the skyline of Hull and the 1981 Humber Bridge (with the longest suspension span in the world).

Kirton-in-Lindsey (OS 112: SK 935983). Beside the B1206 on the outskirts of the town centre.

This site is well hidden on occasions by tree cover.

Willingham Ponds (OS 113: TF 137884). Beside the A631 between North Willingham and Market Rasen.

There is a small refreshment kiosk (open in the summer) and toilets. The Forestry Commission has laid out forest nature trails.

Legbourne (OS 122: TF 366847). Beside the A157 at the Louth end of the village, and next to the Legbourne Railway Museum.

There are toilet facilities.

Lincolnshire Showground site (OS 121: SK 967782). By the junction of the A15 and A1500 roads, 5 miles (8 km) north of Lincoln.

There are toilet facilities. Avoid the show days: the third Wednesday and Thursday in June.

Tattershall (OS 122: TF 204571). Beside the A153 about a mile from the village centre and castle, and opposite the leisure park.

It has a refreshment kiosk (open in the summer) and is partly situated on the trackbed of the former Boston to Lincoln railway line (1848-1959).

Stickney (OS 122: TF 348576). Former railway station site beside the A16.

This has toilets. The so-called 'New Line' crossed the east and west fens between 1913 and 1970.

Huttoft Car Terrace (OS 122: TF 543787), **Moggs Eye**, Huttoft (OS 122: TF 546776), **Wolla Bank**, Anderby (OS 122: TF 556756) and **Chapel Six Marshes**, Chapel St Leonards (OS 122: TF 558741).

These four sites are in a line on the edge of the North Sea and can be reached by side lanes off the main A52 Mablethorpe to Skegness coastal road. At very low tides the remains of a prehistoric petrified forest can sometimes be visited. Only Wolla Bank has no toilets.

Pilgrim Fathers' Memorial, Fishtoft (OS 131: TF 362402).

It is located down narrow lanes just a mile from the village and marks the point of departure of this famous group of Puritans in 1607.

East Bank Lighthouse, Sutton Bridge (OS 131: TF 493256).

Drive along the *right* bank of the river Nene towards its confluence with the Wash. The lighthouse (not open to the public) is associated with the conservation carried out here by the late Sir Peter Scott. There are no toilet facilities.

4
Archaeological sites

Because of the intensive agriculture carried on in Lincolnshire many archaeological sites are inaccessible to the public. Only those with easy access or rights of way are listed here.

Neolithic

There are numerous long barrows scattered along the Wolds, but many are discernible only by aerial photography. Only one can be easily seen and appreciated by the visitor. This is beside the A16 between Louth and Spilsby at the northern end of **Swaby** (TF 372776). It is 257 feet (78 metres) long and at its broadest 64 feet (19.5 metres) wide. The only long barrow in the area to have been scientifically excavated was one of a pair near Skendleby called Giant's Hills. This yielded portions of charred wood which were dated by the carbon-14 method to between 3500 and 2700 BC. Although overgrown by trees, the shape of a long barrow in the middle of a ploughed field beside the A153 near **Tathwell** (TF 295823), between Louth and Horncastle, can be seen from the roadside.

Bronze age

Many of the bronze age round barrows have been ploughed out, in most cases without proper excavations. Of the surviving ones the two best groups to see are those at **Bully Hills** (on the Haugham to Tathwell road at TF 330826) and the group known as **Butterbumps**, just south of the Willoughby-in-the-Marsh to Cumberworth road at TF 494724. The former consists of six barrows, the largest of which still measures 10 feet (3 metres) in height. The latter group contains at least eleven barrows, some of which have been excavated in recent years, and carbon-14 dates of 1750 BC (plus or minus 180) have been obtained from finds.

Iron age

Hillforts

There are three principal iron age hillforts in Lincolnshire, but none of these has been scientifically excavated in the twentieth century. **Honington** hillfort lies on the so-called **Jurassic Way** prehistoric ridgeway, which ran along Lincoln Edge or Cliff. It lies to the south of the village near Grantham and on the

Bully Hills round barrows can be seen on the skyline from the lane that leads from Haugham to Tathwell on the Wolds.

further side of the A153 Grantham to Sleaford road (SK 954424). It appears to guard not only the early trackway but also the Ancaster Gap in the higher land. Roughly rectangular, it measures 375 feet (114 metres) by 430 feet (131 metres). The defence works consist of double banks and ditches. The only visible entrance is near the south-eastern corner.

To the south-east of Grantham near the B1176 Bourne road lie **Ingoldsby Round Hills** (SK 992308), enclosing 2 acres (0.8 hectare) within a near circular earthwork.

Yarborough Camp lies in a wood on the west side of the B1211 near the village of Croxton (TA 082120) and guarded the Kirmington Gap in the northern part of the Wolds. It covers 2³/4 acres (1.1 hectare) and has yielded both iron age artefacts and a hoard of fourth-century Roman coins. In Danish times it was probably the moot (meeting place) for the Yarborough wapentake of local government.

Trackways

As well as the Jurassic Way, there were three other important ridgeways that may date from the iron age. **Barton Street** started in the Lindsey Marshes to the south of Louth and ran along the eastern foothills of the Wolds in a north-westerly direction to the Humber in the region of Barrow-upon-Humber. Parts of it are still in use today, such as Fanthorpe Lane (Louth) at TF 323880 and the A18 road from Wyham (near Ludborough) to Laceby Cross-roads, thence along the A18 to Keelby and the B1211 to Ulceby (although there are diversions on the B1211 due to emparking at Brocklesby).

Starting from the A16 at Calceby (TF 398752) the **Bluestone Heath Road** climbs to the summit of the Wolds and sweeps in a great shallow curve crossing the A153 at Cadwell Park, the A157 near Welton-le-Wold and the A631 at Calcethorpe.

High Street (B1225) must have been used by the Romans as it joins their settlements at Horncastle and Caistor. It keeps fairly constantly to the 490 foot (150 metre) contour. It probably linked with Barton Street at its northern end, near Humberside Airport.

There are round barrows on both the further side of the A153 Grantham to Sleaford Bluestone Heath Road (TF 252919) and High Street (TF 173923).

Roman period

Roman roads

There are several Roman roads that are still in use today. The most famous of these are the A15 north of Lincoln (**Ermine Street**) and the A46 (**Fosse Way**) between Lincoln and Newark. Another section of Ermine Street still in use is the B6403 between Byards Leap (near Cranwell) and Colsterworth. **King Street**, which was a branch of Ermine Street serving the edge of the Kesteven Fens, runs in a straight line between West Deeping and its junction with the present A15 at Kate's Bridge (TF 107147) to the south of Bourne. To the north of that town there is another Roman branch road still in use. Called **Mareham Lane**, it leaves the A15 just south of Aslackby (TF 092294) and runs to Old Sleaford. It is also believed that the B1200 from Saltfleetby to Manby is on the agger (or bank) of a Roman road used for transporting salt inland from pans on the coast. A good walk along a disused section of the Roman road that linked Lincoln with the Wash near Burgh-le-Marsh can be taken between High Street (TF 225775) and its junction with the A153 (TF 272762).

Minor towns

Of three smaller Roman towns in Lincolnshire, only the south ditch and rampart remain of **Ancaster**, a few fragments of fourth-century walls near St Mary's church and in the public library in **Horncastle**, and even more elusive and crumbling remnants at **Caistor**.

Lincoln

The much reconstructed and restored **Newport Arch** guarded the northern exit of Ermine Street from *Lindum Colonia*, as the Romans called the city, and the excavated and preserved remains of the **East Gate** can be seen in the grounds of the Eastgate Hotel, near the east end of the cathedral. Along **East Bight** is a section of excavated wall as well as the base of a water tank. A 70 foot (21 metre) section still stands 3 feet (1 metre) thick and 18 feet (5.5 metres) tall in Westgate and is known as the **Mint Wall**. Along **Bailgate**, set in the

The Newport Arch was the northern entrance to the Roman city of Lincoln.

road surface, are the bases of a monumental colonnade. These are all remains of the settlement for ex-servicemen that was established in about AD 96 on the site of a 41 acre (16.6 hectare) fortress built by the Ninth Legion in about AD 48. The walled town was later extended to occupy a further 100 acres (40 hectares) on the southern slopes of the hill on which the cathedral and castle now stand. The west gate of this extension can be seen in the grounds of City Hall in Orchard Street.

Roman canals

From Brayford Pool (which gives Lincoln the first element of its name, *Lindis*, referring to a pool) to Torksey on the river Trent runs **Fossdyke**, the oldest canal in England still in use. It was dug by the Romans. There are substantial remains, still used in parts for drainage, of a second canal, known as **Car Dyke**, which joined the river Witham with the Glen, the Welland, the Nene and eventually the corn-growing Fens around Cambridge. Its main purpose was probably as a drainage channel rather than for transport. Its presence is preserved in place names such as Dyke (a hamlet north of Bourne) and Car Dyke Farm (TF 112244) in the neighbouring parish of Morton.

Anglo-Saxons and Danes

Few tangible remains can be found of the Anglo-Saxon settlers of the fifth and sixth centuries, apart from place-name evidence and a few excavated cemeteries such as **Welbeck Hill** (near Laceby) and **Loveden Hill** (near Hough-on-the-Hill).

Down a narrow lane on the north side of the A151 on the outskirts of Moulton stands the **Elloe Stone** (TF 313247), which is believed to have been used to mark the site of the moot of Elloe wapentake in Danish times. However, it is unlikely to be in its original location.

At Brotherhouse Bar on the A1073 to the south of Cowbit stands **St Guthlac's Cross** (TF 260149). Traditionally this is said to have been erected by Abbot Thurketyl in the early tenth century to mark one of the boundaries of the lands of Crowland Abbey. Some authorities believe that it is of Norman date.

As well as Anglo-Saxon churches at **Barton-upon-Humber**, **Ropsley** and **Stow**, there are many Saxon church towers and fewer naves. Perhaps the best examples may be seen at St Peter-at-Gowts and St Mary-le-Wigford in **Lincoln** (nave and tower), **Bracebridge** (nave), **Hough-on-the-Hill** (tower) and **Scartho** (tower).

5
Ancient monuments

Bardney Abbey, Bardney (OS 121: TF 113705).

An Anglo-Saxon foundation dating from the end of the seventh century, Bardney Abbey was destroyed by the Vikings and refounded in 1087. It became one of the most important monasteries in Lincolnshire and held considerable property. Although no standing masonry survives, the outlines of the church and other buildings can be seen as earthworks. Finds from the site can be seen at the display centre in Bardney village.

Barlings Abbey, Lincoln (OS 121: TF 090735). 7 miles (11 km) east of Lincoln, off A158.

A Premonstratensian abbey founded in 1154, Barlings was implicated in the Lincolnshire rising of 1536, following which the abbot and four canons were executed. All that remains above ground is a tall fragment of the nave of the abbey church but there are extensive earthworks.

Bolingbroke Castle, Old Bolingbroke, Spilsby (OS 122: TF 349649). 16 miles (25 km) north of Boston, off A16. English Heritage.

Open any reasonable time.

Originally built by William de Roumare, Earl of Lincoln, in the reign of William I, and rebuilt by Ranulph de Blunderville in Henry III's reign, it had by 1363 passed into the hands of John of Gaunt, Earl of Lancaster, who extended it as a royal residence. Here on 3rd April 1367 the future Henry IV (Henry Bolingbroke) was born. It fell into decay after its capture by the Parliamentarian army in October 1643. The site has interpretation panels with reconstruction drawings.

Henry Bolingbroke is commemorated in the village with a bed of red Lancaster roses, given by the Mayor and people of Provins, where the rose originated.

Castle Bytham, Little Bytham, Stamford (OS 130: SK 991185). Private.

This eleventh-century castle was partly destroyed in 1221 after an unsuccessful revolt against the government of Henry III by William de Fortibus, Count of Aumale. It was rebuilt but ceased to be used after the fourteenth century. Although no masonry can be seen, the impressive earthworks tower over this small Kesteven village.

Crowland Abbey, Crowland. (Also known as Croyland Abbey.)

Nothing remains of the original abbey founded by St Guthlac at the beginning of the eighth century. The present parish church of Saints Mary, Bartholomew and Guthlac consists of the north aisle of the massive medieval abbey church. Much more existed of the original nave until the Parliamentary bombardment of the town in 1643. The south aisle was dismantled in the eighteenth century. Nevertheless the visitor can still see something of the abbey's former grandeur from the ruinous west front of the nave and from its eastern extremity marked out in the churchyard.

'Julian's Bower', Alkborough (OS 106: SE 880217).

This is the romantic name for a turf maze which was cut into the grass on a cliff top overlooking the mouth of the Trent, possibly by monks in the twelfth century. The design is repeated in the floor of Alkborough church.

Kirkstead Abbey, Kirkstead, Woodhall Spa (OS 122: TF 190617). Off the B1191.

All that remains above ground is a towering piece of masonry that was once part of the south-east angle of the south transept of this Cistercian abbey church, founded in 1187. There are, however, very substantial earthworks, from which the positions of the church

Kirkstead Abbey, near Woodhall Spa, was a Cistercian foundation.

and cloister can be made out. To the north there is a magnificent series of medieval fishponds.

Nearby is the slightly later St Leonard's church, which stood by the abbey gatehouse to serve the local population. It is amongst the finest examples of mid thirteenth-century ecclesiastical architecture in Lincolnshire.

Lincoln Castle, Lincoln. Telephone: 01522 511068. Lincolnshire County Council. *Open daily.*

On the orders of William I 166 houses were pulled down to make way for Lincoln Castle. Its walls enclose an area of 6¼ acres (2.5 hectares) and it is built on a huge bank 30 feet (9 metres) high and in places 250 feet (76 metres) broad. Of this Norman construction only the gateway (refronted in the thirteenth century), an observatory tower and the Lucy Tower remain. Cobb Hall was added to the north-east corner in the thirteenth century. In the bailey stand the former prison, built in

1787, and the Law Courts (1826). There is also the bust of George III which was rescued from the toppled figure that graced the top of the Dunston Pillar to the south-east of the city from 1810 until 1940. The castle featured in the two battles of Lincoln: it was held by King Stephen against his cousin Matilda (2nd February 1141) and by Henry III's forces against the Dauphin Louis of France (21st May 1217). In the Civil War it was captured by Parliamentarians in 1644. The old West Gate has been excavated and reopened.

Scredington packhorse bridge (OS 130: TF 097409)

At the hamlet of Northbeck is this two-arch bridge spanning the North Beck, a short distance from the Roman Mareham Lane.

Somerton Castle, Boothby Graffoe, Lincoln (OS 121: SK 954598). Private.

Situated at the foot of Lincoln Edge near Boothby Graffoe (A607), Somerton Castle

South Kyme Tower was built by Sir Gilbert de Umfraville in the mid fourteenth century.

The remains of St Leonard's Priory, Stamford.

was built on Welsh garrison lines by Anthony Bek in 1281, while he was still Bishop of Durham (he was translated to Lincoln for a few months in 1320). It covered an area 330 by 180 feet (101 by 55 metres). Here in 1356 King John II of France was imprisoned while awaiting the payment of his ransom. Of the medieval castle only the south-east tower and a portion of the curtain wall remain; the rest dates from Elizabethan times.

South Kyme Priory, South Kyme, Lincoln (OS 130: TF 168499). Beside the B1395 to the east of Sleaford.

In 1890 the architect Hodgson Fowler restored a fragment of the priory church of the Augustinian canons which had been on this site since before 1169. Although basically a Victorian church, it still has a feel of the monastic about it.

In the meadow near it stands South Kyme Tower, a four-storey ashlar tower 77 feet (23.5 metres) high, built on the orders of Sir Gilbert de Umfraville in the mid fourteenth century.

Stamford: St Leonard's Priory, Priory Road, Stamford.
Accessible at all times.

St Leonard's Priory was founded as a Benedictine house in 1082. The west front and north arcading of the priory church, dating from the early part of the twelfth century, still stand in an accessible meadow. Edward I is known to have stayed here when passing through the town.

Sutton St James: St Ives Cross (OS 131: TF 388182).

Near the west end of the main village and on the B1165 on a small triangular green

stands quite a substantial medieval cross, the shaft of which is supported by a trio of buttresses. Tradition has it that it was used by local women as a base from which to sell their dairy products to passers-by.

Tattershall Castle, Tattershall, Lincoln LN4 4LR. Telephone: 01526 342543. National Trust.
Open: April to October, Saturday to Wednesday and bank holiday Mondays; November and early December, Saturdays and Sundays only.

In 1434 Ralph, Lord Cromwell, pulled down the previous castle, which had been

The keep of Tattershall Castle is built of local brick.

erected by Robert de Tateshall in 1231, and had the present structure in locally fired red brick built in its place. Both the brickmaker and the principal bricklayer appear to have been Dutch. Standing six storeys high (including the basement), it reaches a height of 110 feet (33.5 metres) and is rectangular in section, 87 by 67 feet (26.5 by 20.5 metres).

Temple Bruer (OS 121: TF 008539). To the north of the road that joins A607 at Welbourn with A15.

Situated in the middle of a farmyard, the 54 feet (16.5 metres) high tower, which in the thirteenth century formed the south chancel tower of the round church of the Holy Sepulchre, was restored in 1961. The preceptory of the Knights Templars was founded in the reign of Henry II by William Ashby (of nearby Ashby-de-la-Launde?). In 1833 the main church was excavated and found to have had a diameter of 52 feet (16 metres).

Thornton Abbey (OS 113: TA 115190). Near Barrow-upon-Humber, beside the minor road to East Halton. English Heritage.

These massive monastic remains are of the Augustinian Thornton Abbey founded near the banks of the Humber in 1139. The gatehouse was probably started in 1382, stands 68 feet (21 metres) high and is constructed partially of red brick and partially of ashlar. It is approached by a causeway 120 feet (36.5 metres) long across the moat and with contemporary brick walls and turrets. Excavations have revealed the foundations of the mighty church, started in about 1264, which was 282 feet (86 metres) long (including a later Lady Chapel of 1395). Parts of the dormitory, chapter-house and refectory are also visible. Some of the robbed ashlar can be seen in the walls of the nearby Abbey Farm.

The church tower at Temple Bruer.

The gatehouse at Thornton Abbey.

Tupholme Abbey, Lincoln (OS 121: TF 143681). Near Bardney beside the B1190.

The south wall of the refectory of the Premonstratensian abbey founded about 1160 stands between two deserted farmhouses. It includes a very fine reader's pulpit, used while the monks ate their meals in silence.

Utterby packhorse bridge (OS 113: TF 305932).

Down Church Lane and near St Andrew's church are the sideless remains of a cobbled packhorse bridge carried on a single chamfered arch, and probably dating from the fourteenth century.

West Rasen packhorse bridge (OS 112: TF 063893).

Near the thatched post office stores beside the A631 is a narrow fifteenth-century bridge over the little river Rase, and consisting of three ribbed arches.

The reader's pulpit at Tupholme Abbey.

6
Churches

There were in the late middle ages over a thousand parish churches and manorial chapels in Lincolnshire as it was then constituted. Even today, with so many closures and the virtual disappearance of the chapel of ease, the diocese of Lincoln contains hundreds of places of worship. In addition nonconformity has found a stronghold in this area. To the seventeenth-century Baptists, Independents (Congregationalists) and Quakers were added the eighteenth-century Methodists. When they split between the Wesleyans, Primitives and Frees early in the nineteenth century even more chapels were created, so that at the time of the unique Religious Census of March 1851 there were 1500 places of worship within the historic confines of Lincolnshire. In this chapter only a tiny percentage of them can be examined.

Binbrook: St Mary and St Gabriel. (Northeast of Market Rasen, on B1203.)

In this village there were originally two separate parishes, but by 1840 St Gabriel's was a ruin (its site is marked by a single small reconstructed pillar on a grassy bank beside the B1203), whilst St Mary's could only be described as 'dilapidated'. It was the Louth-based architect James Fowler who designed the present handsome ironstone church to replace the other two in 1869, using an Early English style of architecture. Its broach spire is more reminiscent of Kesteven than the heart of Lindsey. The fourteenth-century font bowl was retained, however, as was the complete medieval cross by the south porch. Until the base closed down at the end of the 1980s, it was also the station church for RAF Binbrook, and there are several reminders of this long association in the church.

Boston: St Botolph.

Dedicated to an East Anglian missionary who died in 680, the present magnificent church dates from the fourteenth century. The steeple was begun in 1309 and reaches a height of 272 feet (83 metres), paid for out of the port revenues from the export of wool. Known locally as 'the Stump', it is said to have been roughly based on the Belfry at Bruges, with which Boston had medieval trading connections. The top section is in the form of a lantern (similar to the ones at Ely

Cathedral and Greyfriars in King's Lynn) for the guidance of shipping. The total length of the church is just 10 feet (3 metres) more than the height of the Stump, and the building covers 20,070 square feet (1866 square metres), making it the fourth largest parish church in England. Although many of the fittings inside are Victorian in date, they include a 1612 pulpit, Georgian wrought-iron communion rails, some fine late medieval brasses and an inscribed Tournai marble slab to the memory of the Hanseatic merchant Wissel Smalenburg, who died in 1340.

Bourne Abbey: St Peter and St Paul.

The only house of the Augustinian canons of the Arrouasian Reform was at Bourne. Although all other traces of the monastic connections, apart from blocked-up arches of the north wall of the church of Saints Peter and Paul, have disappeared, the abbey church still remains as it was rebuilt about 1200. Originally twin west towers were planned, but only one was constructed. One of the church's prized possessions is a 1742 brass chandelier. In the late thirteenth century Robert Manning, the author of *A Chronicle of England* and one of the first translators of books from French into English, was a canon here.

Brant Broughton: St Helen. (East of Newark, north of A17.)

This parish church possesses the fourth

The Friends' Meeting House at Brant Broughton.

highest steeple in Lincolnshire, at 198 feet (60 metres). The interior is kept in immaculate condition, and when the chancel was rebuilt in 1876 the then rector (Canon F. H. Sutton) designed the stained glass himself, and C. E. Kempe executed the work. The ironwork also was produced locally.

Brant Broughton: Friends' Meeting House.

In Meeting House Lane stands the simple place of worship dating from 1701, with its horse-mounting block *in situ*. Its original fittings are preserved. At the rear is a typical Quaker cemetery, which is still in use.

Burgh-le-Marsh: St Peter and St Paul. (West of Skegness, on A158.)

Apart from the 1702 south porch, this is a Perpendicular-style church. The tower has a strikingly painted clock face that was originally intended for the nearby Market Place. Inside there is a fine carved pulpit of 1623, whilst the lectern was carved in 1874 by Jabez Good, a local barber, antiquarian and author of a book on marshland dialect that is still in print. In the south-west corner of the nave are relics from the former St Paul's Missionary College, which existed nearby from 1868 until the mid 1930s to train Anglican priests for overseas work.

Deeping St James: St James. (Just east of Market Deeping, south of A16.)

In Deeping St James church is this graveside shelter for use by the minister during inclement weather.

This parish church was originally the priory church of a Benedictine house founded as a cell of Thorney Abbey in 1139. However, its tower dates only from the first half of the eighteenth century. The remainder of the church is a mixture of the Norman, Early English and Decorated styles. There are a Norman tub-shaped font and two fourteenth-century effigies. There is also one of those graveside shelters that were used in the nineteenth century to keep vicars dry during burial services in wet weather.

Freiston: St James. (East of Boston, south of A52.)

Freiston is a coastal village and this Perpendicular church began life attached to the Benedictine priory that adjoined it, founded by Alan de Craon as a cell of the great Crowland Abbey in 1114. As Arthur Mee so rightly declares, 'the most striking feature of the exterior is the clerestory, with eight great windows on each side'. Inside there are the remnants of the original church dating from the Norman period, with twelfth-century zigzag motifs. However, some of this 'Norman' work, such as one of the doorways, is as recent as 1871, when James Fowler carried out some restoration work.

Gedney: St Mary Magdalene. (East of Holbeach, south of A17.)

Standing in the middle of an elongated parish stretching some 9 miles (14 km) from Gedney Drove End on the shores of the Wash to Gedney Fen, this magnificent medieval church can be seen across the fields from the A17 near Long Sutton. One of its glories is the Perpendicular-style clerestory and, since there is no stained glass in the church, on a sunny day the light floods into the interior. Although spireless, the tower itself is an imposing 86 feet (26 metres) tall. One of the most delightful artefacts inside is the brass in the south aisle depicting a lady who died *c*.1400, with a puppy shown at her feet.

When built, the spire of St Wulfram's, Grantham, was the tallest on an English parish church.

Grantham: St Mary (Roman Catholic).

Built in North Parade in 1832, St Mary's stands opposite the shop where Margaret Thatcher lived and grew up. In the classical style, the church is faced with ashlar and has a charming little cupola. Roman Catholics have an unbroken tradition in Grantham. The Blessed Hugh More was born in the town in 1563 to Protestant parents but chose to go to Rheims to train for the Catholic priesthood. He returned to England on the eve of the Armada in 1588 and was hanged at Lincoln's Inn Fields in London.

Grantham: St Wulfram.

When the steeple was completed in 1300 it was taller than any other building in England, at 272 feet (83 metres). Although it lost its record as regards parish churches to St James's, Louth, two centuries later, the actual tower, at 196 feet (60 metres), is some 46 feet (14 metres) taller than that at Louth. Although the Victorian glass inside makes it rather dark, there are some modern windows, including one to the Porter family, who have been in the shoe trade in the town for generations. Within the tower is a chained library of 150 volumes, donated in 1598 and containing a legal book printed in Venice in 1472. It is sometimes open to the public.

Grantham: Finkin Street Methodist Church.

Off the High Street stands this imposing edifice of 1840 with its twin towers, which Pevsner likens to the pavilion built by Sir John Vanbrugh in the early eighteenth century in the grounds of Swinstead Old Hall, a few miles away. Its pillared entrance is equally impressive. Inside there is a capacious balcony. One item of especial interest is the lectern, dedicated to Alderman Alfred Roberts, a Methodist local preacher and father of Margaret Thatcher, who worshipped here as a girl.

Heckington: St Andrew. (East of Sleaford, south of A17.)

This is one of the largest parish churches in Lincolnshire, being 164 feet (50 metres) long and 85 feet (26 metres) wide. Externally the most notable features are the number and intricacy of the pinnacles and the seven-light east window with its wealth of tracery. Inside, the jewel is the Easter sepulchre, with its carvings of sleeping soldiers, a mermaid and

a bagpiper. The medieval churchyard cross has been restored.

Helpringham: St Andrew. (South-east of Sleaford, on B1394.)

In the summer of 1972 this church achieved national fame when its tower and broach spire were selected for the 7$^{1}/_{2}$p stamp in a new series on English churches, in preference to those of nearby Ewerby and Heckington, both of which had taller steeples. Its spire is typical of many medieval Kesteven churches with its crocketing and two tiers of lucarnes (openings). The font (*c.*1200) is of interest in that one side depicts a bird, a quadruped and what may be the Tree of Life. In contrast there is a triptych painted by A. E. and P. E. Lemon in 1940; these artists are also responsible for some of the church's modern stained glass.

The crocketed spire of Helpringham church.

Lincoln Cathedral viewed over the rooftops in the Bail quarter of the city.

Langton-by-Partney: St Peter and St Paul. (North of Spilsby, west of A16.)

Probably built between 1720 and 1730, this is one of the most perfect examples of Georgian ecclesiastical architecture and fittings in Lincolnshire. Built of dark red brick, it has an unusual octagonal belfry and broad overhanging eaves. Inside there are box pews, a fine gallery and one of the few three-decker pulpits to survive in this area. The church is to be found down a lane on the west side of the A16 near Partney.

Lincoln Cathedral

Situated in one of the most dramatic positions of any English cathedral, the present building has an overall length of 481 feet (147 metres) and covers an area of 57,200 square feet (5313 square metres). Dedicated to the Blessed Virgin Mary, it stands partly on the site of the first-century Roman fortress. This is the third cathedral to have stood here. The first, consecrated in 1095, was destroyed by fire in 1141. The second was shattered by an earthquake on Palm Sunday, 1185.

The rebuilt central tower collapsed again in

1230 and was replaced by the present one, 268 feet (82 metres) high. Until it collapsed in the reign of Elizabeth I, it was surmounted by a top-heavy spire of 250 feet (76 metres), making the whole structure a massive 518 feet (158 metres) high, some 114 feet (34.5 metres) taller than that of Salisbury Cathedral. The west front is the only portion of the Romanesque first cathedral still standing. This has been restored in recent years because of the action of acid rain, probably from the nearby Trent power stations. It has tier upon tier of statuettes of kings, saints and bishops.

It was St Hugh of Avalon (Bishop from 1186 to 1200), who began the post-earthquake rebuilding. In 1255 Henry III was petitioned to allow the city wall to be breached so that the cathedral could be extended eastwards. Another famous medieval Bishop of Lincoln, Robert Grosseteste (1235-53), is buried in the mid thirteenth-century south transept, which also contains the large but later round window known as the Bishop's Eye (*c.*1330). The north transept is the setting for the complementary Dean's Eye window. One of the chief glories of the cathedral is the Angel

Choir, completed in 1280, with its comprehensive set of medieval misericords, along with the famous Lincoln Imp (to be found on the north side, high on the penultimate pillar before the high altar is reached). When the choir was completed, the remains of St Hugh were translated to a new shrine in the presence of Edward I and Queen Eleanor.

Edward I was also present in the chapterhouse for sessions of Parliament in 1284 and 1301, whilst his son called Parliament to meet here in 1315 and his grandson in 1329. Here the trial of the Knights Templar took place in 1310, and the leaders of the Lincolnshire Rising assembled in October 1536 to hear the reply of Henry VIII to their requests. The ten-sided plan also incorporates a frieze telling Old Testament stories. The fine library designed by Sir Christopher Wren in 1674 is nearby, as is the cathedral's restaurant.

Louth: St James.

Built from the profits of the local wool and cloth industry, St James's possesses the tallest spire of any parish church in England, at 295 feet (90 metres), which far exceeds the church's total length of 182 feet (56 metres). This steeple was completed in Ancaster stone in 1515, and visitors can climb to the base of the spire on summer afternoons to obtain a panoramic view over the town and the Lindsey Marshes to the coast. Inside, the chancel arch contains the blocked stairs that led to the rood loft. In the north-east corner stands the Sudbury Hutch, an early Tudor chest. The interior is comparatively light. The minute heads on the exterior windows of the south aisle include those of a recent rector and a headmaster of the King Edward VI School. The Lincolnshire Rising began here on 1st October 1536.

Louth: Methodist Church.

Although this is the oldest Methodist church in the town, it has outlasted all the others, which have since been closed, demolished or converted to secular purposes. In 1836 it was erected on Eastgate (although its present entrance is on Nichol Hill) as the Wesleyan Centenary Chapel. In its original form it could seat up to 1600 worshippers, by means of tightly packed box pews and a large oval gallery. But in 1977 the whole of the interior was stripped, the gallery pulled down and the church completely modernised. At the same time, to strengthen the walls, several windows had to be blocked in. Later, the sculptor Noel Black produced a remarkable work consisting of five large polished steel panels on which is mounted the Bible story from the Creation to Pentecost, with especial emphasis on the events of Holy Week.

Market Rasen: Centenary Wesleyan Church.

At the top of Union Street, cheek by jowl with the railway station, stands the 1863 Methodist Church. Its imposing front consists of a quartet of Ionic pillars supporting a pediment. The rest of the exterior is of red brick with stone quoins, with two tiers of windows. Inside are the original box pews, oval gallery and double-decker pulpit.

Marton: St Margaret. (South of Gainsborough, near junction of A156 and A1500.)

A modern carving on St James's church, Louth, depicting Canon Aidan Ward, a former rector.

Standing beside the busy A156, but also near the line of the the Roman Tillbridge Lane (Lincoln to York highway), the eleventh-century church has relics of its Roman connections with red tiles incorporated in the herringbone style of its late Anglo-Saxon tower, which still displays the original roofline of the nave. Other parts of the church have been modernised, such as the Perpendicular windows, but basically this building is one of the best extant examples of this phase of ecclestiastical architecture.

Pickworth: St Andrew. (South of Sleaford, west of A15.)

Hidden down lanes in a small Kesteven village, this church has some of the finest medieval wall paintings to have been found in this part of England; they date from c.1380. Amongst other themes are the Doom over the chancel arch, the Ascension and St Christopher on the north wall of the nave, and the Weighing of Souls on the north arcade. However, since they were revealed by Clive Rouse in 1950, they have unfortunately begun to fade, and reproductions of them when freshly discovered give a better idea of their original colours.

Sempringham: St Andrew. (At OS 130: TF 107329, west of B1177 near Billingborough.)

Sempringham was the birthplace of St Gilbert, who in 1139 became the only Englishman to found a monastic order. Of the monastery and its huge church nothing remains, but of the parish church, where St Gilbert himself was vicar, the Norman nave and south doorway remain from his time. The centrally placed tower is basically fourteenth-century and the present chancel dates only from 1869. St Gilbert's original community of seven nuns lived in a cell attached to the outside of the north wall of the nave.

Snarford: St Lawrence. (6 miles, 10 km, north-east of Lincoln, west of A46.)

A narrow lane leads from the A46 down to this small church, which contains the most magnificent set of family monuments in Lincolnshire. These are of the St Paule (Pol) family, who lived in an adjacent mansion,

since demolished. The alabaster memorials date respectively from 1582, 1613 and 1619 and take a variety of forms.

South Somercotes: St Peter. (North-east of Louth, west of A1031.)

Referred to as the 'Queen of the Marshes', this fine stone church was declared redundant in 1986 and, after a certain amount of restoration work, has been in the hands of the Redundant Churches Fund since then. Its fifteenth-century spire is the only one on a village church in this area between Louth and the coast and was one of the few to be damaged by enemy air activity in the Second World War. The village's name is a reminder of how in medieval times it would have provided summer pasturage for flocks of sheep from elsewhere (for example Great Coates on the Humber estuary). Sheep can still be seen grazing the churchyard in the summer.

Stow: St Mary. (At SK 882820, south-east of Gainsborough, on B1241.)

This magnificent, spacious, early eleventh-century parish church dominates the undulating country east of the river Trent. The crossing under the central tower measures 26 feet (8 metres) in width and 30 feet (9 metres) in height. It had fallen into a ruinous state by the Norman Conquest, so that Remigius, the first Bishop of Lincoln, had it rebuilt with a Norman chancel, which made the building 150 feet (46 metres) long. The church was restored in 1853-64. St Hugh of Avalon, Bishop of Lincoln from 1186 to 1200, lived in nearby Stow Park with his pet swan.

Tattershall: Holy Trinity. (South-west of Horncastle, on A153.)

Commissioned by Lord Treasurer Ralph Cromwell in 1440, the church took forty years to complete. Constructed of Ancaster stone, probably floated down the rivers Slea and Witham, it is 186 feet (57 metres) long and is beautifully light and airy inside. Here the visitor can see the brass of its creator, although the heads of Ralph and his lady are missing. Amongst other brasses are those of two priests belonging to the college that was attached to Holy Trinity.

The Bishop's Eye rose window in Lincoln Cathedral.

The library and colonnade built by Sir Christopher Wren in Lincoln Cathedral cloisters.

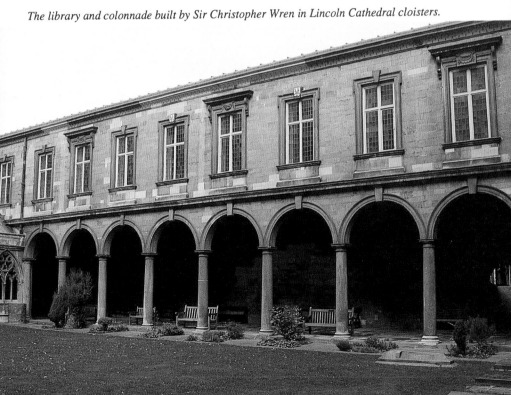

7
Historic houses and gardens

Aubourn Hall, Aubourn, Lincoln LN5 9DZ. 7 miles (11 km) south of Lincoln.
Open: July and August, Wednesday afternoons.
This Elizabethan house with a fine staircase is set in attractive gardens currently being restored and improved.

Belton House, Belton, Grantham NG32 2LS. Telephone: 01476 66116. North of Grantham on the A153/A607. National Trust.
Open: end of March to end of October, Wednesday to Sunday and bank holidays.
Sir Nikolaus Pevsner, the architectural historian, described Belton House as 'perhaps the most satisfying among the later seventeenth-century houses in England'. From the reign of Elizabeth I until 1980 it was the home of the Brownlows; the founder of the dynasty was a judge in the Court of Common Pleas. However, the present house was largely designed by William Stanton between 1685 and 1689. Ancaster stone, quarried at nearby Heydour, was used in its construction. It was restored by James Wyatt in 1777. Much of the interior, such as the marble hall and the tapestry room, dates from *c.*1722, although the library was part of Wyatt's contribution.

The small accompanying parish church of Saints Peter and Paul contains many of the monuments of the Brownlows and their ancestors the Custs. Some of these are in a special mortuary chapel added in 1816 and designed by Sir Jeffry Wyatville.

The boundary wall of Belton Park stretches for 5 miles (8 km), enclosing an area of 700 acres (283 hectares). During the First World War part of this was used as a temporary army camp. In 1750 a tall arch known as the Belmount Tower was erected and this dominates the parkland laid out by William Eames. An adventure playground for children has been constructed in the north-west corner of the grounds. Belton was acquired by the National Trust in 1983.

Burghley House, Stamford PE9 3JY. Telephone: 01780 52451. On the B1443, 1 mile

Burghley House, near Stamford. The famous Horse Trials are held in the park each September.

Doddington Hall is a late Elizabethan mansion to the west of Lincoln.

(1.6 km) south-east of Stamford.
Open: April to the first Sunday in October, daily.

Although most of Burghley Park is strictly within the county of Cambridgeshire today, it has dominated the life of the Lincolnshire town of Stamford since the sixteenth century. The estate was purchased by David Cecil in 1528, but it was his grandson, Sir William Cecil, Queen Elizabeth I's chief minister, who enlarged the existing house. The first section of the new Burghley House was built between 1556 and 1564 and included the great hall, the vast kitchen and the stone staircase on the north front. The second building phase started in 1577 and included the clock-tower (dated 1585).

Burghley is truly a 'treasure house', containing one of the finest private collections of seventeenth-century Italian paintings in the world, including works by Giordano, Gentileschi, Preti and Liberi. The Italianate ceilings of some of the state rooms are stun-ning in their three-dimensional effects. There are superb English and continental tapestries, many of which have been recently conserved. Burghley also houses the earliest inventoried collection of oriental porcelain in the west. As well as exhibits of the craftsmanship of workers from the school of Grinling Gibbons and the finest English furniture makers, there is a massive 3000 ounce (85 kg) silver wine cooler and many of the athletic trophies won by the late sixth Marquess of Exeter, including his 1928 gold medal for hurdling.

The extensive parkland was designed and laid out by Lancelot 'Capability' Brown in the late eighteenth century. The Burghley Horse Trials are held here each September.

Doddington Hall, Doddington, Lincoln LN6 4RU. Telephone: 01522 694308. On the B1190 5 miles (8 km) west of Lincoln.
Open: gardens, mid March and April, Sunday afternoons; house, May to September, Wednesday, Sunday and bank holiday afternoons.

Belton House, near Grantham.

Opposite: Crowland's parish church is the former north aisle of a much bigger abbey church.
The beautiful gardens at Burghley House.

Built for William Fydell in 1726, Fydell House in South Street, Boston, is now a university extramural centre.

This Elizabethan house was built for Thomas Taylor, registrar to the Bishop of Lincoln between 1593 and 1600. The architect was Robert Smithson, who was also responsible for Longleat and Hardwick Hall. The house still stands as it was built, with its walled gardens, gatehouse and family church. The hall is built from locally manufactured bricks and has Ancaster stone dressings.

During the Civil War it was the home of the Royalist Sir Edward Hussey, whose son was killed fighting in the battle of Gainsborough in 1643. On the other hand, since there were marriage connections with the Parliamentarian general Lord Fairfax, Doddington was spared spoliation by both sides!

The formal gardens are probably the best in Lincolnshire. Meals are served in a licensed restaurant in the grounds of the hall.

Epworth: The Old Rectory, 1 Rectory Street, Epworth DN9 1HX. Telephone: 01427 872268.
Open March to October, Monday to Saturday and on Sunday afternoons.

The rectory to which the Reverend Samuel Wesley and his wife, Susanna, came in 1696 was burnt first in 1702 and then in a more serious fire in 1709 by local residents who disliked his outspoken preaching. It was rebuilt incorporating the ribs and keels from ships broken up in the nearby river Trent. Locally produced reeds and plaster were combined to make hard, fire-resistant floors.

John Wesley was born here on 17th June 1703 and Charles Wesley on 18th December 1707. Some rooms are now set out in period style with furniture of the type that the brothers would have known, together with some of their belongings. There are also collections of portraits, prints and Methodist pottery. Over-night accommodation is available.

Fulbeck Hall, Lincoln Road, Fulbeck, Grantham NG32 3JW. Telephone: 01400 272205.
Open at Easter and bank holiday Mondays, as well as daily in August.

The original home of the Fane family was burnt down in 1731 and rebuilt in the style of a Stamford town house, on to which various later additions have been made. Inside is a collection of Dutch, Italian and English oil paintings, and watercolours by General Walter Fane, painted in the nineteenth century. An Arnhem Exhibition, in one of the rooms unrestored since the Second World War, commemorates the use of the house as headquarters of the 1st Airborne Division from 1943 to 1945. The gardens were laid out in 1905 and include a Venetian well.

Fydell House, South Street, Boston PE21 6HU. Telephone: 01205 351520.
Open during university terms, Monday to Friday.

Built in 1726, probably by William Sands of Spalding, for William Fydell, the house is now used by the Department of Adult Education of Nottingham University as an outpost. The interior decor is in the rococo style of the mid eighteenth century and includes panels of plasterwork on the stairway and a frieze in the corridor. The exterior of the house has tall Doric pilasters and an equally imposing Doric columned doorway with a scrolled open pedi-

ment. There is a small but pleasant garden at the rear of the building.

Gainsborough Old Hall, Parnell Street, Gainsborough DN21 2NB. Telephone: 01427 612669. Situated near the shopping centre of the town.
Open throughout the year, Monday to Saturday (except Good Friday, Christmas and New Year) and on Sunday afternoons from Easter to October.

The original mansion of Sir Thomas Burgh was burnt down by the Lancastrian army in 1470. He rebuilt it in red brick and entertained Richard III here in 1484. Of this house, the hall, north-east turret and kitchen block survive. Between 1597 and 1600 William Hickman, a London merchant, extended the building, and the east and west ranges of the extension remain. When in about 1720 the Hickman family built a new seat nearby at Thonock, the Old Hall passed through bad times. Although not abandoned, it was used for such diverse purposes as a linen factory, a theatre, a public house, a Congregational chapel and even as living accommodation in

Gainsborough Old Hall.

Prize cattle at the 1994 Lincolnshire Show.

Opposite: Heckington tower mill is unique in retaining its eight sails. Combining on a farm at Great Carlton, near Alford.

the form of flatlets. In 1952 the building was leased to the Friends of the Old Hall. The building is run jointly by Lincolnshire County Council and English Heritage.

The hall has strong connections with non-conformist dissent, especially with John Smyth, the 'Sea Baptist', and, a century later, John Wesley.

Grantham House, Castlegate, Grantham NG31 6SS. Telephone: 01909 486411.
Open: April to end of September, Wednesday and Thursday afternoons.

The *National Trust Guide* describes Grantham House as 'that agreeable pheno-menon, a country house in a town'. According to Sir Nikolaus Pevsner, the oldest parts of the building (windows situated now on an internal staircase) date from *c.*1380. This is all that remains of the house in which Princess Margaret, future wife of James IV of Scotland, and Cardinal Wolsey, briefly Bishop of Lincoln in 1514, stayed. Most of the present Grantham House dates from the sixteenth, seventeenth and eighteenth centuries. The chimney stack bears the date 1574; the garden front can be dated on architectural evidence to about 1680 but is known to have been remodelled in 1737. Inside there is contrasting early seventeenth-century oak panelling in one room and painted panelling from the following century in the drawing room. The most recent restoration was carried out by the architect Lawrence Bond when he lived here in the early twentieth century.

Grimsthorpe Castle, Grimsthorpe, Bourne PE11 0NB. Telephone: 01778 591205. On the A151 between Bourne and Colsterworth.
Open: Easter Sunday to end of September; Sundays, Thursdays and bank holidays; August, daily except Fridays and Saturdays.

Grimsthorpe Castle has been the ancestral home of the Willoughby family since they moved from Eresby, near Spilsby, in Tudor times. Until his death in 1983 the family was headed by the third Earl of Ancaster, who has been succeeded by his daughter Jane as twenty-seventh Baroness Willoughby de Eresby, there being no direct male descendants to inherit the earldom.

The castle stands in what were originally the grounds of the Cistercian abbey of Vaudey, founded in 1147. In the late thirteenth century a castle was built nearby by Gilbert de Gant. Katherine, daughter of the tenth Baron Willoughby de Eresby, married Charles Brandon, Duke of Suffolk, brother-in-law to Henry VIII. They moved to Grimsthorpe and began to develop the site into a magnificent mansion, which the king himself visited in 1541. Incorporated was some of the medieval castle, including the so-called King John's Tower, which forms the south-east corner of the present building. Since the sixteenth century the north front has been successively remodelled in 1685 and in 1727 (by the poet-architect Sir John Vanbrugh). Vanbrugh was also responsible for the long hall, which measures 110 feet (33.5 metres). The west front was redesigned in 1811.

The parklands consist of some 3000 acres (1200 hectares). They were landscaped by Lancelot 'Capability' Brown in 1772, although the formal gardens and military bastions were the work of George London. The Lincolnshire Trust for Nature Conservation has close connections with the park through nature trails and the gift shop.

Gunby Hall, Gunby, Spilsby PE23 5SS. Telephone: 01909 486411. By the junction of A158, A1028 and B1196, 6 miles (10 km) west of Skegness. National Trust.
Open April to September: house, Wednesday afternoons only; gardens, Wednesday and Thursday afternoons only.

In 1944 the National Trust acquired Gunby Hall and its 1400 acres (567 hectares) of parkland and farmland, although it remained the home of Lady Diane Montgomery-Massingberd until her death in 1963. The Massingberds have been associated with Gunby since medieval times. In 1700 Sir William Massingberd had the present hall erected in local red brick with stone quoins and dressings, designed in the style of Sir Christopher Wren. In 1873 a two-storey extension was built on to the north side, and this matches the 1700 building very well. Beyond that there is the 1735 coach-house, sur-

Gunby Hall, near Skegness, built in 1700, now belongs to the National Trust.

mounted by a 1778 clock-tower, brought from Hook Place in Hampshire in 1917. Inside the hall are family portraits, including some by Sir Joshua Reynolds, and mementoes of visits by Dr Samuel Johnson and Alfred, Lord Tennyson to Gunby.

Beyond the walled garden (with its charming little rotunda) lies St Peter's church, which was rebuilt by James Fowler in 1871. It contains brasses to two earlier members of the Massingberd family (*c.*1400).

Harlaxton Manor, Harlaxton, Grantham NG31 9EY. Telephone: 01476 64541.
Open by appointment only, as it is the British Study Campus of the United States University of Evansville, Indiana.

Gregory Gregory, in the days when he lived at Hungerton Hall (also near Grantham), took a great amateur interest in architecture. When he acquired the decaying seventeenth-century Harlaxton Manor, he decided to demolish it and erect a palatial mansion reflecting his own whims, based on ideas he had gleaned from visits to many other great

houses. The final eccentric mixture of styles appears to have been a combination of his own views and those of William Burn and Anthony Salvin. The building is approached from the A607 by an impressive drive that dips to a bridge and then climbs to a Tudor-style gatehouse, between amply walled kitchen gardens.

Harlaxton Manor Gardens, Grantham NG32 1AG. Telephone: 01476 592101.
Open April to October, Tuesday to Sunday and bank holiday Mondays.

The elaborate gardens that surrounded Harlaxton Manor are now being restored to their original Victorian splendour, including canal, colonnade, conservatory and terraces.

Lincoln: Bishop's Palace, Minster Yard, Lincoln. Telephone: 01522 553135. English Heritage.
Open April to September, daily.

The Old Bishop's Palace was begun *c.*1163 by Bishop Robert Chesney, from whose episcopate is dated the East Hall. Bishop Hugh de Welles completed the West Hall *c.*1224. However, the major feature that stands restored and open to visitors (often with exhibitions in it) is the Alnwick Tower, built by the bishop of that name in the mid fifteenth century. Unfortunately in 1648, during a siege in the Civil War, much of the palace was reduced to ruins. However the Alnwick Tower was reconstructed in 1867. It is now administered by English Heritage. The palace of the Bishops of Lincoln has at other periods been situated at Nettleham and Riseholme to the north of the city.

Marston Hall and Gardens, Marston, near Grantham NG32 2AY. Telephone: 01400 50225.
Open occasional summer Sundays or by appointment.
Marston has been held by the Thorold family since the fourteenth century but after damage in the Civil War the chief seat of the

Woolsthorpe Manor, the birthplace of Isaac Newton, and an apple tree descended from the tree that inspired the discovery of the law of gravity.

baronet was moved to Syston nearby. Marston was reduced in size and Georgian rooms were formed within the Great Hall. It contains many interesting pictures, and furniture made by Gillow for the family.

Normanby Hall and Country Park, Scunthorpe DN15 9HU (OS 112: SE 855167). Telephone: 01724 720588. 4 miles (6 km) north of Scunthorpe, off B1430.
Park open daily all year. House open April until September, daily, afternoons only.
Normanby Hall was built in 1825-30 as the home of the Sheffield family by Robert Smirke in the Cubic style. It was extended in 1906-8 by Walter Brierley of York. A large east wing was added, containing a dining room, and a north wing housing the servants' quarters. The north wing was demolished in 1949. The hall has been decorated and furnished in the style of the Regency period. Displays include eight period rooms, a temporary exhibition gallery and costume galleries.
See also Normanby Park Farming Museum, page 98.

Woolsthorpe Manor, Colsterworth, Grantham NG33 5NR. Telephone: 01476 860338. National Trust.
Open April to October, Wednesday to Sunday afternoons and bank holiday Monday afternoons.
The house where Sir Isaac Newton was born on Christmas Day 1642 is a stone-built yeoman farmer's house of *c.*1620, with low ceilings and some fine examples of Jacobean woodwork. There are also examples of moulded chimneypieces. It has hardly been altered since the days of Newton's childhood and contains some memorabilia of the famous scientist and mathematician, such as his telescope. The garden contains a descendant of the famed apple tree said to have inspired him to the discovery of the law of gravity.

Opposite: Stamford Brewery Museum in All Saints Street tells the story of brewing in the town.

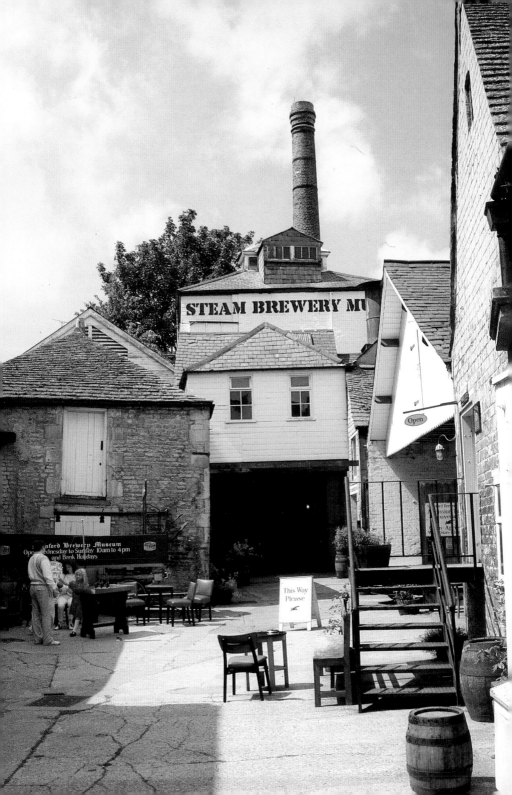

8
Museums

Alford

Alford Manor House Museum, West Street, Alford LN13 9DL. Telephone: 01507 466488 or 463073.
Open daily.

This thatched building, said to have been erected in 1661, was restored by the Alford Civic Trust and is used as a local museum. It shows aspects of the domestic and commercial life of Alford as well as the links between Alford and the USA. Agricultural implements and machinery are shown in buildings behind the house.

Mawthorpe Museum, Mawthorpe, Alford LN13 9LU. Telephone: 01507 462336. On the B1196 south of Alford.
Open June to September, Wednesdays and Thursdays; also Tuesdays from mid July to third week in August and some Sundays from June to September.

This is a private collection made up principally of items to do with farming and rural life. There is a Marshall steam roller of 1923, a Foster portable steam engine made as late as 1942 and a 1918 threshing machine by the same Lincoln manufacturer. There is a static display of tractors covering the period 1932 to 1954. In addition there are various 'departments' with exhibitions of items dealing with butchery, wash days, tin smithing, carpentry, and so on, along with relics from the East Lincolnshire railway line that used to run at the rear of the premises.

Barton-upon Humber

Baysgarth Museum, Baysgarth Park, off Caistor Road, Barton-upon-Humber DN18 6AH. Telephone: 01652 632318.
Open Thursday to Sunday and bank holidays (except Christmas period).

This Georgian house contains period rooms and displays of geology, archaeology, local history, military history, country crafts and local industries. There is also a fine collection of European and oriental pottery and porcelain. The museum has changing temporary exhibitions.

Boston

Boston Guildhall, South Street, Boston PE21 6HT. Telephone: 01205 365954.
Open Monday to Saturday throughout the year and on Sunday afternoons from April to September. The rest of the year closed on Sundays, Christmas and New Year.

The chief exhibits are connected with the Pilgrim Fathers, whose cells can be seen, along with a kitchen equipped as it would have been in the early seventeenth century. The building itself dates from the fifteenth century but has been modified over the intervening centuries.The rooms on the first floor were refurbished in the early Georgian period. The Maritime Room contains many local shipping and fishing artefacts.

Coningsby

The Battle of Britain Memorial Flight Visitor Centre, Dogdyke Road, Coningsby LN4 4SY. Telephone: 01526 344041.
Open Monday to Friday (except bank holidays and Christmas/New Year period).

Guided tours are made around the hangar at Royal Air Force Coningsby which contains the famous Lancaster, Hurricane, Dakota and five Spitfires. A visitor centre has a small exhibition, video material and a souvenir shop.

Cranwell

Cranwell Aviation Heritage Centre, Heath Farm, North Rauceby, Sleaford. Telephone: 01529 488490. Situated just off the A17 on the other side of the road to the RAF College.
Open daily (except on Christmas Day and New Year's Day).

This centre records in words and photo-

The Manor House in West Street, Alford, houses the local museum.

graphs the story of the nearby Royal Air Force College, as well as those of surrounding air bases both past and present.

Dorrington

North Ings Farm Museum, Dorrington, Lincoln LN4 3QB. Telephone: 01526 833100. Off the B1188 at the Musicians' Arms, through the village and under a railway bridge to a right turn to the farm.
Open Easter to October, Sundays only.

Agricultural machinery, a collection of vintage tractors, a narrow-gauge railway and a small foundry make up this private museum.

East Kirkby

Lincolnshire Aviation Heritage Centre, The Airfield, East Kirkby, Spilsby PE23 4DE. Telephone: 01790 763207. Beside the A155.
Open Monday to Saturday (except Christmas period).

This collection based on the old control tower is devoted to the history of Lancaster Squadrons 57 and 630. Items on display include cockpits from Canberras, a Shackleton and an Avro Lancaster, military vehicles and photographs.

Grantham

Grantham Museum, St Peter's Hill, Grantham NG31 6PY. Telephone: 01476 68783. Lincolnshire County Council.
Open all year, Monday to Saturday.

As well as exhibits connected with the lives of Sir Isaac Newton and Margaret Thatcher, this museum also contains some excellent display cabinets dealing with the prehistory of the area and a case covering the history of the manufacture of road rollers in the town by the firm of Aveling & Barford. There is a fine collection of Roman ironwork recovered from the site of the Saltersford waterworks upstream from the town.

Grimsby

National Fishing Heritage Centre, Alexandra Dock, Great Grimsby DN31 1UZ. Telephone: 01472 344868.
Open daily (except 25th and 26th December and 1st January).

The Lawn, Lincoln, once a mental institution, now houses a number of visitor attractions.

The Usher Gallery in Lincoln holds important collections of decorative art.

Here visitors can experience the drama of the high seas, sign on and take a journey to the Arctic fishing grounds and back again, take a tour around the trawler *Ross Tiger* and experience the special exhibition 'The Poseidon Experiment'.

Back O'Doigs Museum, Alexandra Dock, Grimsby DN31 1HZ. Telephone: 01472 344868.
Open daily.
Changing displays of local life and history.

Hemswell

Bomber County Aviation Museum, Hemswell Cliff, Gainsborough DN21. Telephone: 01482 215859. Situated at the former RAF Hemswell base beside A631 (OS 112: SU 948889).
Open weekends.
Opened as an RAF station in 1937 and closed in 1967, this museum displays several aircraft, including a Canberra, a Hawker Hunter, and a Bristol Sycamore helicopter.

Immingham

Immingham Museum, Margaret Street (Resource Centre), Immingham DN40 1LE. Telephone: 01469 577066.
Open Monday to Friday, and Saturday mornings.
The main theme is the role of the Great Central Railway Company in the development of the town's docks and railway.

Legbourne

Legbourne Railway Museum, The Old Station, Legbourne, Louth LN11 8LH. Telephone: 01507 603116. Situated beside the A157.
Open Easter to end of September, Tuesday to Sunday and bank holidays.
A working signal box and restored country station on the former East Lincolnshire Coast Railway house a model railway and almost two thousand items of railwayana.

Lincoln

Lincoln Centre for Archaeology, The Lawn, Union Road, Lincoln LN1 3BL. Telephone: 01522 560330.

Open daily.
This permanent display, guarded by a life-size model of a Roman legionary, explains graphically how an archaeological excavation takes place, with life-size models performing various tasks.

Lincolnshire Road Transport Museum, Whisby Road, Doddington, Lincoln LN6 0QT. Telephone: 01522 500566 or 689497. 3 miles (5 km) south-west of the city centre, just off the B1190.
This collection of vehicles includes a 1909 horse-drawn hearse, a 1927 Dennis 4 ton lorry, a 1930 Singer Junior car, a 1941 Merryweather fire engine and a 1948 Guy 'Arab III' double-deck bus, amongst other vehicles. In addition there are static displays of old-style road signs, bus conductresses' uniforms and ticket equipment and early bus timetables.

Museum of Lincolnshire Life, The Old Barracks, Burton Road, Lincoln LN1 3LY. Telephone: 01522 528448. Lincolnshire County Council.
Open daily (but closed Sunday mornings October to April).
This, the region's largest social history museum, housed in the 1857 barracks of the North Lincoln Militia, contains displays illustrating community life, domestic life, crafts and trades and the Royal Lincolnshire Regiment. It also has a fine collection of locally built agricultural machinery and an industrial section. Its largest exhibit is a 1909 Ruston-Proctor steam navvy. There is a regular programme of temporary exhibitions and craft demonstrations. It is only ten minutes' walk from the cathedral and is close to the castle.

National Cycle Museum, The Lawn, Union Road, Lincoln LN1 3BU. Telephone: 01522 545091.
Open daily (except for Christmas week).
This museum tells the story of the cycle from the hobby horse, through the velocipede and the penny-farthing, to some of the classic machines of the twentieth century, including the locally built Lincoln 'Elk' and the 11 feet (3.4 metres) tall 'Eiffel Tower' bicycle, as well as many cycling artefacts.

Church Farm Museum, Skegness.

Usher Gallery, Lindum Road, Lincoln LN2 1NN. Telephone: 01522 527980.
Open Mondays to Saturdays, and Sunday afternoons (except Christmas, New Year and Good Friday).
Built in Temple Gardens in 1927, the gallery contains glass, porcelain, miniatures, Tennyson mementoes and examples of locally produced pottery such as Torksey ware, as well as housing pictures. There is a significant topographical collection, including works by Peter de Wint and Turner. James Usher himself was a watchmaker and there is an interesting collection of both clocks and watches on show.

Louth

Louth Museum, 4 Broadbank, Louth LN11 0EQ (off Northgate). Telephone: 01507 601211 or 604717.
Open March to November, Wednesday, Friday, Saturday and Sunday afternoons; also every day in August.
Outside this small museum is a 4¹/₂ ton erratic boulder which was carried to the area by glaciation from the Cheviots in Northumberland, and which until 1827 served as a borough boundary stone. Inside can be found a varied collection of local items, including a

prize-winning carpet woven locally, models of small boats built at Riverhead for the defunct Louth Navigation, artefacts and photographs connected with the excavations of the Cistercian Louth Park Abbey, and some displays of natural history, fossils and domestic items.

Metheringham

Airfield Visitor Centre, Westmoor Farm, Martin Moor, near Metheringham, Lincoln LN4 3BQ. Telephone: 01526 378270.
Open during the spring and summer at weekends. Telephone for details.
The story of 106 Squadron, Bomber Command, RAF, and Metheringham Airfield during the Second World War is here told in photographs, documents and memorabilia.

Normanby

Normanby Park Farming Museum, Normanby Hall Country Park, Normanby, Scunthorpe DN15 9HU. Telephone: 01724 720588.
Open April to September, every afternoon.
This museum was opened in 1989 and houses displays of traditional agricultural equipment and rural crafts. It was extended in 1993 with the addition of a transport gallery,

education facilities and a rural industries gallery.

Sandtoft

Sandtoft Transport Centre, Belton Road, Sandtoft DN8 5SX. Telephone: 01302 842948 (24-hour information line: 01724 711391). 3 miles (5 km) west of Belton on the Isle of Axholme (OS 112: SE 748081).

On a former wartime airfield at Sandtoft there is a collection of trolleybuses from such places as Aachen, Bradford, Cleethorpes, Liege, Nottingham, Reading, South Shields and Walsall. On certain days members of the public can ride on some of these vehicles round the double circuit of overhead wiring that has been erected outside the large depot. On occasions special buses are run to Sandtoft from Doncaster.

Scunthorpe

Scunthorpe Borough Museum and Art Gallery, Oswald Road, Scunthorpe DN15

Ayscoughfee Hall, Spalding.

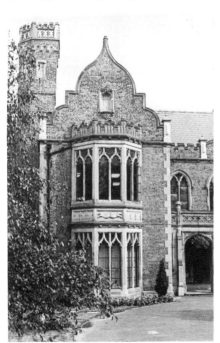

7BD. Telephone: 01724 843533. Scunthorpe Borough Council.
Open Tuesdays to Saturdays, and on Sunday afternoons.

Situated next to Frodingham church, this acts as the regional museum for the area. Its wide-ranging modern displays deal with the region's history and wildlife. Of particular note is the archaeological gallery, which reflects the richness of the area's heritage. Incorporated in the museum building is a Victorian ironworker's cottage.

Skegness

Church Farm Museum, Church Road South, Skegness PE25 2ET. Telephone: 01754 766658. Lincolnshire County Council.
Open Easter to the end of October, daily.

The former farmhouse and ancillary buildings of Church Farm, dating from the middle of the eighteenth century, form the nucleus of an expanding collection of agricultural and domestic bygones. A typical east Lincolnshire 'mud and stud' cottage from the village of Withern was re-erected here in 1982. In 1985 a brick and pantile barn was dismantled at Havenhouse and re-erected on the site, its upper granary floor being converted into a temporary exhibition gallery.

South Witham

Geeson Bros Motorcycle Museum and Workshop, Water Lane, South Witham, Grantham NG33 5PH. Telephone: 01572 767280 or 767386.
Telephone for opening dates and times.

There are eighty-six motorcycles here, some dating back to 1913, and including Ariel, Brough Superior, Campion, Humber, Hesketh (prototype), Rudge Whitworth and Swallow.

Spalding

Ayscoughfee Hall and Gardens, Churchgate, Spalding PE11 2RA. Telephone: 01775 725468. South Holland District Council.
Open daily except winter weekends.

Ayscoughfee Hall is the museum of South Holland District, with galleries on drainage and land reclamation, agriculture and horticulture, village and Spalding history. The

Geest Gallery has regular temporary exhibitions. Ayscoughfee Hall also houses part of the cased bird collection for the Spalding Gentlemen's Society.

Stamford

Museum of Almshouse Life, Browne's Hospital, Broad Street, Stamford. Telephone: 01780 63746.

In 1987 two of the medieval rooms were opened, the lower to show various aspects of almshouse life, the upper housing various temporary exhibitions.

Stamford Brewery Museum, All Saints Street, Stamford PE9 2PA. Telephone: 01780 52186.

Open March to September, Wednesday to Sunday, and on bank holidays (when it will be closed the following Wednesday).

Although Stamford's brewing industry was not as extensive as in other towns in the East Midlands, for many years the town had two thriving breweries. In this museum many aspects of the story of brewing in Stamford are graphically told.

Stamford Museum, Broad Street, Stamford PE9 1PJ. Telephone: 01780 66317. Lincolnshire County Council.

Open all year, Monday to Saturday; also Sunday afternoons from April to September.

The museum interprets the historic town of Stamford for the visitor. Amongst the main exhibits are examples of Stamford ware, a green-glazed cream fabric pottery which was manufactured in the town from late Saxon times (*c.*850) until the middle of the thirteenth century. In a later period Stamford produced terracotta ware (1858-75) and also

built Pick cars (*c.*1899-1925). The famous fat man Daniel Lambert, who died at Stamford, is depicted by a life-sized model.

The museum also publishes six *Town Trails* describing the historic architecture of the town.

Stickford

Allied Forces Military Museum, Main Road, Stickford, Boston PE22 8ES. Telephone: 01205 480517.

Open Monday to Saturday.

This is a display of many types of British and American army vehicles and other wartime exhibits.

Whaplode St Catherine

Museum of Entertainment, Millgate, Whaplode St Catherine, Spalding PE12 6SF. Telephone: 01406 540379. On the B1165.

Open: Easter to end of June and in October, Saturdays, Sundays and bank holidays; July to September, Monday to Friday afternoons and all day on Saturdays and Sundays.

A registered charity, this private collection of mechanical music apparatus through the past two centuries includes disc music boxes, player pianos and all kinds of organs, including one from the Gaumont Cinema, Coventry. There is also a collection of phonograph and gramophone records.

Woodhall Spa

Cottage Museum, Iddesleigh Road, Woodhall Spa. Telephone: 01526 353775.

Open Easter to October, daily.

This traces the history of how a chance discovery of mineral springs in the early nineteenth century, when prospecting for coal, led to the foundation of this spa resort.

9
Industrial archaeology

Alford Tower Mill, Alford (OS 122: TF 457765). Telephone: 01507 462136. On the A1104 near its junction with the A1111.
Open March to September, Saturdays and bank holidays; also on other days (telephone for times).

This windmill was known as Hoyle's Mill and was built by Sam Oxley, an Alford millwright, in 1837. Tuxford's of Boston supplied the machinery. There are five sails and six floors, the third floor having an external gallery. It is at this level that there are four pairs of stones, three for grinding provender and one for wheat flour. The mill ceased to work commercially in 1955. It was bought by the County Council and renovated and is now back in full commercial operation.

Algarkirk Woad Mill (OS 131: TF 246342).

Situated down a lane off the A17 is a set of buildings that were used as Lincolnshire's last static woad mill until the 1930s. Before the introduction of synthetic dyes woad was grown over a considerable acreage in the Fens (hence Woad Lane, Sutton Bridge, and Woad Farm School, Boston). Its culture is mentioned by Arthur Young in his 1813 account of agriculture in the county, especially at Brothertoft, to the west of Boston. As well as permanent sites, such as the one here at Algarkirk, there were mobile woad mills that operated in the Holbeach Drove area of the Fens until the Second World War.

Alvingham Mill, Alvingham, Louth LN11 0PZ (OS 113: TF 365913). Telephone: 01507 327544.
Open August and September, second and fourth Sundays, and Mondays and Thursdays.

It is known that a watermill existed here in 1155, when the Gilbertine house was established next to it. It is fed by the river Lud, the

Alvingham Mill on the river Lud has a breast wheel.

Cogglesford Mill, Sleaford.

present mill dating from the eighteenth century. It is unusual in that it has a breast wheel (the incoming water hits the paddles halfway up the wheel). Now restored to working condition, Alvingham Mill grinds provender (feed for cattle and horses), although baking flour, ground elsewhere, is on sale.

Boston: Maud Foster Mill, Willoughby Road, Boston (OS 131: TF 331448). Telephone: 01205 352188. Beside the Maud Foster Drain in the centre of Boston, and clearly seen from the A16 and the B1183, which runs along the opposite side of the Drain.
Open all year on Wednesday, Sunday and bank holiday afternoons.

This is a five-sailed windmill and dates from 1809. Its main claim to fame is that some of the original experiments for developing Reckitt's Blue were carried out on the premises. It is commercially operated and there is a shop on the premises.

Burgh-le-Marsh Tower Mill, Burgh-le-Marsh, Skegness (OS 122: TF 503650). Tele-

phone: 01754 810609 or 766658. On the A158, 5 miles (8 km) west of Skegness.
Open second and last Sunday of every month; other times by arrangement.

Known as Dobson's Mill, this mill was built by Oxley of Alford *c*.1813. It has five sails and five storeys, the third containing three pairs of stones. Another pair was installed on the second floor, to be operated by a diesel engine (since removed). The mill ceased to work commercially in the early 1960s. Subsequently it was bought by the County Council and is open to visitors. This mill differs from most others in that it has left-handed sails.

Cogglesford Watermill, East Road, Sleaford. Telephone: 01529 414294.
Open May to October, daily; November to April, Saturdays and Sundays.

The eighteenth-century mill, house and outbuildings stand by the first of the locks on the Slea Navigation. The mill has been restored to working order and houses an exhibition about its history.

Dogdyke Steam Pumping Station, Bridge Farm, Tattershall Bridge, Lincoln (OS 122: TF 199565). Telephone: 01526 342352. Approach along a private road at Bridge Farm, on the south side of the A153 near Tattershall Bridge.

Here is the last working steam drainage engine in the Fens. Erected in 1856, the beam engine drained, by means of a wooden scoop wheel, several thousand acres of surrounding fenland. In 1940 it was replaced by a Ruston & Hornsby diesel engine, which is also now preserved.

Gainsborough: Britannia Works (OS 112: SK 818898).

Beaumont Street is graced by the façade of Marshall's Britannia Works, much of which dates from 1850, when Lincolnshire's thriving engineering industry was beginning to expand. The symbolic figure of Britannia surmounting this frontage is a reminder of how firms like Marshalls led the world with their products such as steam engines and, later, tractors. William Marshall had founded his enterprise in 1848, and by 1904 the works were employing no less than 3600 men. In 1880 the works also became a technical institute, where engineering, mechanical drawing and machine construction were taught by Marshall's chief draughtsman, Mr Gibbs.

Gayton Engine, near Theddlethorpe All Saints (OS 122: TF 453881).

This small yellow brick pumping station prevented flooding by the nearby Great Eau when it was opened in 1874. It has been lovingly restored by volunteers and is likely to be opened to the public in the near future.

Grimsby Dock Tower (OS 113: TA 278112).

J. W. Wild's Dock Tower of 1851-2, at 303 feet (92 metres), is the tallest structure in South Humberside and was designed in the Italianate style, taking one million bricks to construct. Its base is 28 feet (8.4 metres) square. Its hydraulic machinery was constructed by Sir William Armstrong and worked the main lock gates. It is now disused. Originally there were three smaller hydraulic towers, but only one of these survives. The largest lock controlled by the big tower was 70 by 300 feet (21 by 91 metres) and the adjacent one for barge traffic was 45 by 200 feet (13.6 by 60 metres).

Grimsby: Victoria Mill, Victoria Street, Grimsby (OS 113: TA 272096).

This massive structure on the banks of the haven by Corporation Bridge was built in stages in 1889 and 1906. It is in Flemish style and is one of the largest flour mills remaining in the area.

Heckington Tower Mill, Heckington, Sleaford (OS 130: TF 147437). Telephone: 01529 60765. On the B1394 by Heckington railway station.

Open Saturday and Sunday afternoons throughout the year; Thursday and Friday afternoons from Easter to third week in July. Other times for groups by arrangement.

This magnificent windmill is the only surviving one with eight sails in Britain. As originally built by Michael Hare in 1830 it had five sails. However, in about 1890 the cap and sails were wrecked in a storm. A replacement cap and eight new sails came from Tuxford's Mill in Boston. The sail area was now over 1500 square feet (139 square metres), giving the mill more than average power. There are five floors. The five pairs of stones are spread over three of these. However, there were never enough hands available to work them all at the same time. The mill ceased commercial work in 1942 and was acquired by the County Council in 1953 and opened to the public.

Kirton-in-Lindsey: Mount Pleasant Windmill (OS 112: SK 938995). Telephone: 01652 640177. Beside B1398 north of the town.

Open all the year round on Saturdays, Sundays and bank holidays and on weekdays in July and August.

Built in 1875, this mill was wind-powered until 1936 when its sweeps were removed. It was restored between 1987 and 1991, a new cap and sails being fitted. It is now a working mill producing stoneground flour, and the complex includes a mill shop and tea shop.

Lade Bank Pumping Station, near Sibsey (OS 122: TF 380546).

When John Rennie was given the formidable task of draining the huge East Fen to the north of Boston in 1805, he built the Lade Bank Pumping Station on the banks of the Hobhole Drain. This was added to in 1867 by the erection of the present main block with its tall chimney.

Lincoln: Ellis' Mill, Mills Road, Lincoln (OS 121: SK 971722). Telephone: 01522 546422. Lincoln Civic Trust.
Open May to September, Saturday and Sunday afternoons; alternate weekends from October to April.

This small four-sail tower mill is the last survivor of a line of eight such mills on the west side of the city, on Mills Road. In 1973 it was gutted by fire but four years later it was acquired by the Lincoln Civic Trust. It has

since been fully restored, using machinery from other mills, and is open to the public at weekends, grinding corn when the wind permits. The new sails are 3 feet (0.9 metre) shorter than the originals, to avoid problems for tall visitors. It has three floors and two pairs of stones.

Lincoln: St Mark's Railway Station, High Street (OS 121: SK 973708).

When the new spur line was opened in 1985 diverting trains from Newark and Nottingham into Lincoln Central Station, St Mark's was closed. However, since it was Lincolnshire's first town station (being opened by the Midland Railway in 1846) it was decided not to demolish its entrance with its Ionic portico and fluted columns. So this was shored up, whilst after the rails were removed the trackbed was excavated to reveal the location of the medieval Carmelite friary.

Ellis' Mill, in the middle of Lincoln, is fully operational once more.

Louth: Eve's Carpet Factory, James Street (OS 122: TF 373877).

A blue plaque on an old warehouse proclaims that this was part of a manufactory where Adam Eve (an unknown child survivor from a local shipwreck) began to weave carpets *c.*1707 in a former woollen factory. He employed around sixty adults and children. In 1867 one of his carpets was highly commended at the Paris Exhibition. Two carpets of *c.*1850 are exhibited in the Louth Museum, Broadbank. The site was once more extensive, stretching down to the banks of the Lud. It was renovated in 1994.

Louth Riverhead (OS 122: TF 340881).

Some of the late eighteenth-century warehousing along the basin of the Louth Navigation still stands. The canal itself was opened on 20th May 1790 and stretched 12 miles (19 km) to the North Sea at Tetney Lock. In all there were eight smaller locks on its first 3 miles (5 km) out of Louth, with unusual curved sides. Vessels left weekly for Grimsby and Hull and monthly for London (hence the adjacent street name of Thames Street). The canal itself was closed to traffic in 1924, but the river Lud still flows along its course.

New Bolingbroke: The Crescent (OS 122: TF 309580).

After the successful draining of Wildmore and West Fens by means of steam pumps, John Parkinson founded the industrial settlement of New Bolingbroke (on the present B1183) in 1824 with a view to weaving bombazine (a twill mix of worsted, silk and cotton) and crepes. Although this enterprise was at first successful, he went bankrupt in January 1827, causing the mill to close. The Crescent with its two-and-a-half storey central section was built to house the plant and some of the workforce, the rest living in the terraces of cottages on either side of the complex. The Wesleyan Methodist chapel was built for their spiritual needs in 1825, predating by a quarter of a century St Peter's church.

New Holland: Manchester Square (OS 112: TA 083239).

When the Manchester, Sheffield & Lin-

Maud Foster is a five-sailed working mill in Boston.

colnshire Railway (nicknamed 'The Mucky, Slow and Late'!) took over the existing ferry to Hull in 1848, it built accommodation for its workpeople: forty-five dwellings on three sides of a grassed square. It also constructed a school and a church (replaced in 1901 by the present Christ Church) and for rail and ferry passengers, the Yarborough Arms Hotel, later renamed the Lincoln Castle. The MS&LR also opened a dock and timber pool. The pier ceased to carry railway tracks when the Humber Bridge was opened in 1981.

Pinchbeck Engine. Telephone: 01775 725468 (OS 131: TF 260258). Off West Marsh Road near Spalding.

Open April to October, daily.

Erected in 1833 to pump dry the surrounding fens, it ceased work in 1952. It drained up to 3,690,000 tons of water during particularly wet years. In 1988 the Welland and Deeping Internal Drainage Board decided to enter into a partnership with South Holland District Council to restore this beam engine and create a land drainage museum.

Pode Hole Pumping Station, near Spalding (OS 131: TF 212220). On the A151 road to Bourne.

The station is still in use, albeit with modern electric engines and a concrete section added early in the twentieth century. However, one of the original massive steam engines installed to drain the local fens in 1825 is still preserved *in situ*.

Sibsey: Trader Mill, Sibsey, Boston (OS 122: TF 344510). Telephone: 01246 822621. About 1 mile (1.6 km) west of Sibsey on A16 beside B1184. English Heritage.
Open on special milling days only. Telephone for details.

This fine six-sailed mill represents the height of windmill technology. It was one of the last to be built in Lincolnshire, being constructed by Saundersons of Louth in 1877, although Saundersons continued building windmills until 1892. Trader Mill ceased commercial operations in 1953 but has since been restored.

Sleaford: Maltings (OS 130: TF 074452).

Situated beside the railway tracks near Sleaford station are the enormous former maltings of Bass. Four pavilions stand on either flank of a four-storey central tower block, which housed the workshops and steam engine. The length of this impressive complex is 1,000 feet (303 metres), and it was completed in 1905 for the brewing firm of Bass, Ratcliff & Gretton Ltd. Unfortunately a fire in the 1970s, along with general neglect, has taken its toll on the largest such set of buildings outside Burton-on-Trent.

Sloothby: Carpenter's Shop (OS 122: TF 493710). Near Willoughby.

The hamlet of Sloothby is situated down a

'Tales of the River Bank' visitor centre tells the story of the draining of the Fens.

lane off the eastern side of the B1196 just south of Willoughby. The carpenter's shop and that craftsman's house stand on the edge of this isolated community on the left-hand side of the lane. The large doors and windows proclaim its industrial purpose, and it was the last such complex to survive in use after the Second World War in this area. It contrasts remarkably with the small former forge at a T junction at the other end of the hamlet. It is now a private dwelling.

Spalding: railway footbridges (OS 131: TF 245231 and 242227).

Standing on either side of the 1848 stock-brick railway station are two of the longest extant iron footbridges in Lincolnshire. The one to the north of the station spanned not only the existing line from Sleaford and the former line from Boston, but about one dozen sidings, used in their final days for excursion trains bringing spectators for the annual Tulip Parade through the streets of the town. The footbridge to the south of the station still spans the Peterborough line but once also spanned those to March and King's Lynn.

Stamford East Railway Station, Water Street (OS 130: TF 035069).

Located in the suburb of St Martin's With-out, this building was designed by William Hurst in 1855-6 for the Great Northern Rail-way, which operated a branch line out to join the East Coast Main Line at Essendine. Since the station was situated on land belonging to the Marquess of Exeter (of nearby Burghley House) it was necessary to build it in local cream-coloured stone and of classical propor-tions, making it the most impressive small terminus in the county. The last passenger train entered it on 13th June 1959.

Stockwith Mill, near Somersby, Spilsby (OS 122: TF 358704). Telephone: 0165 888 221. Situated between Hagworthingham (on the A158) and Harrington.

Fed by Tennyson's brook, this is no longer a working mill. However, visitors can see the undershot wheel *in situ*. The rest of the mill buildings have been converted into a tea room and a craft centre.

'Tales of The River Bank' visitor centre and Timberland pumping station. Tele-phone: 01529 488490. East of Billinghay on the A153; turn north along the bank of the river Witham at Tattershall Bridge. North Kesteven District Council.

Visitor centre open May to October, Wednes-day to Sunday afternoons; November to April, Saturday and Sunday afternoons. Pumping station open occasionally.

The pumping station was built in 1839 to drain the local fens. A beam engine was used originally but in 1924 the existing Gwynne's centrifugal pump was installed. The visitor centre explains the history of the station and the draining of the fens.

Waltham Tower Mill, Waltham, Grimsby (OS 113: TA 260033). Telephone: 01472 827282. Beside the B1203 at the southern end of the Grimsby suburb of Waltham.

Open Easter to September, Sunday after-noons.

Trader Mill at Sibsey is in the care of English Heritage.

Wrawby Post Mill, near Brigg.

Originally (1880) a six-sailer, one pair of sweeps was destroyed in a gale just before the First World War and was not replaced until 1986. This was the last working mill in the area. It is now grinding corn again. Its ancillary buildings have been converted to workshops and a restaurant.

Wrawby Post Mill, Wrawby, Brigg (OS 112: TA 026088). Telephone: 01652 653699. Near the A18 at the eastern outskirts of the village, near Brigg.
Open bank holiday Mondays and the last Sunday in June and July, afternoon only.

This is the last remaining post mill (built 1790) in the area. It was restored to working condition in 1964 but was almost wrecked in a winter gale and had to be restored once more. It has four sails and from time to time, on its windy hilltop site, grinds flour for sale.

10
Other places to visit

Billinghay Cottage and Craft Workshop, Billinghay. Telephone: (Sleaford Tourist Information Centre) 01529 414294. Just off A153 from Sleaford to Horncastle, by the Golden Cross public house.

A typical 'mud and stud' cottage, dating from the seventeenth century has been restored using traditional building techniques. It is limewashed and has a thatched roof. Adjacent to the cottage is a blacksmith's workshop.

Butterfly and Falconry Park, Long Sutton, Spalding PE12 9LE. Telephone: 01406 363833 or 363209. Off the A17 Long Sutton bypass.
Open end of March until end of October, daily.

Here are hundreds of free-flying butterflies inside tropical houses, along with live displays twice a day of falcons, hawks and owls. The 15 acre (6.75 hectare) site also contains

an animal farm centre, adventure playground, wildflower meadows, picnic area and tea room.

Claythorpe Watermill and Wildfowl Gardens, Aby, near Alford LN13 0DU (OS 122: TF 415790). Telephone: 01507 450687.
Open March to October.

Built in 1721, the mill stands on the Great Eau but is no longer milling, being a tourist attraction comprising wildfowl gardens with hundreds of waterfowl and park birds, and the mill with its restaurant, gift and Country Fayre shops.

Covenham Reservoir, Covenham St Bartholomew, near Louth (OS 113: TF 350962).

As well as being a nature reserve with a hide from which various species of duck and other interesting waterfowl can be watched, this is also a recreational area, where, on 25

Billinghay Cottage is a typical fenland cottage, now restored using traditional materials.

The Humber Bridge can be admired from a special viewing area.

acres (10 hectares) of open water sailing and other water sports take place under the auspices of the Covenham Water Sports Association.

Fantasy Island, Ingoldmells, nr. Skegness PE25 1RH. Telephone: 01754 872030.
Open daily.
A new all weather theme park with rides, sideshows, shops and restaurants.

Fenland Aquajets, Spion Cop Farm, Langtoft Fen, Langtoft, near Market Deeping PE6 9QB (OS 130: TF 115115). Telephone: 01778 342236.
Open daily.
60 acres (24 hectares) of fish lake with quads and water-skiing.

Fenside Goat Centre, Chestnut Lodge, Fenside Road, Toynton All Saints, Spilsby PE23 5DD. Telephone: 01790 752452. Off A16 south of Spilsby.
Open: Easter to June, Sunday, Monday and Wednesday afternoons; July and August, daily except Tuesdays and Saturdays.
This is a working dairy goat farm, but it does contain other domesticated stock, including donkeys. There are spinning and weaving demonstrations. Ice cream and cheese made from goats' milk are on sale.

Freshney Park Way, Grimsby.
This is situated along the banks of the river Freshney from Little Coates (OS 113: TA 240091) and the West Marsh area of Grimsby, and covers 300 acres (121.5 hectares) of open space. It caters for anglers, birdwatchers, cyclists and walkers. Picnic tables are also available, and there are ample parking facilities at the Grimsby Leisure Centre along Cromwell Road. A ranger service is available by telephone: 01472 242000.

Hardy's Animal Farm, Anchor Lane, Ingoldmells, Skegness, PE25 1LZ. Telephone: 01754 872267.
Open from Easter until the beginning of October.
This modern working farm has the usual diversity of livestock and a special pig viewing unit. An adventure playground for children is provided, and disabled facilities.

Humber Bridge Viewing Area, Waterside. Barton-upon-Humber (OS 112: TA 028234).
For those who do not wish to cross the Humber Bridge but want just to enjoy its magnificent size and to marvel at its engineering there is an ample car park on the banks of the river with facilities for visitors. The footpath along the Humber bank provides a view of all the water-borne traffic there is at this point (mainly proceeding to and from the inland port of Goole).

Jungle World, Lakeside, Cleethorpes DN35 0AG (OS 113: TA 318073). Telephone: 01472 602118.
Open daily.

This is an indoor tropical garden with mini-beasts from around the world: lizards, tarantulas, exotic insects, birds and more.

Kids Kingdom, Manby Park, near Louth (OS 113: TF 395873). Telephone: 01507 327358. *Open daily.*
This all-weather attraction has a soft play area, bouncing castle, ball pond, swings, etc. There is also a tea bar.

King John's Lost Jewels Trail
The trail, suitable for both motorists and cyclists, covers 23 miles (37 km) of quiet rural roads, starting from Long Sutton Market Place (OS 131: TF 432229). It leads through Gedney Dyke to the edge of the Wash at Gedney Drove End, past King John's Farm, along the banks of the Nene to Sutton Bridge (an area now drained and embanked, but where the royal jewel train was said to have been lost in the quicksands on 16th October 1216). The final leg of this trail is through Tydd Gote and Tydd St Mary (reminders of how far inland medieval tides used to penetrate) back to Long Sutton. An informative map and set of notes are available from South Holland District Council.

Langworth Animal Park and Monkey Sanctuary, Barlings Lane, Langworth, Lincoln LN3 5DF (OS 121: TF 066760). Telephone: 01522 754226. Situated off the A158. *Open daily.*
Rare breeds of poultry and sheep are on display as well as a monkey house. A coarse fishing lake, adventure playground and touring caravan park are also situated here. There is a licensed restaurant and a tea room.

Natureland Seal Sanctuary, North Parade, Skegness PE25 1DB. Telephone: 01754 764345.
Open daily except Christmas and New Year.
Opened in 1965, Natureland concentrates on entertainment, education and conservation, especially of seals, which are rescued

from the Wash when injured or abandoned as pups. There is also a pets' corner and a tropical aviary, where over twenty varieties of butterflies are bred.

North End Animal Gardens, Mablethorpe LN12 1QG (OS 122: TF 499870). Telephone: 01507 473346.
Open Easter until October, daily.
Opened in 1974, the gardens contain over two hundred animals and birds, many associated with the coastline. Seal pups are rescued and restored to health here, as are guillemots, razorbills and gulls. There is also a free-flight aviary and a collection of owls.

Springfields Gardens, Spalding PE12 6ET. Telephone: 01775 724843.
Open April to September daily, and at other times for special events.
Opened in 1966 by the British bulb industry and registered as a charity, the 25 acre (10 hectare) landscaped gardens provide a permanent display centre for spring flowers, particularly tulips and daffodils. From July to September summer bedding and roses can be seen. A forced flower show is held under cover at Springfields in early February and the gardens host the famous Spalding Flower Parade in early May each year.

Tallington Lakes, near Stamford. Telephone: 01778 347000. Beside the A15.
This is a 200 acre (81 hectare) site of water-filled pits used for water sports (with instructors at hand), including sailing, windsurfing and jet-skiing. There are also facilities for fishing.

Tattershall Castle Country Club, Tattershall, Lincoln (OS 122: TF 205575). Telephone: 01526 343193.
Beside the A153 just to the west of Tattershall Castle are water-filled gravel pits with a restaurant, picnic areas, caravan and camping sites, and facilities for canoeing and water sports.

11
The coast

Although Lincolnshire, according to the map, has a long coastline, not all of it is either suitable or available for the visitor to enjoy. For example, there are three aircraft bombing ranges that are in use on most weekdays throughout the year. These are situated at Donna Nook (near North Somercotes), near Wainfleet, and near Holbeach.

The tide in the Humber estuary goes out a long way at **Cleethorpes**, leaving sand flats exposed. These are ideal for donkey rides and beach games, but not for swimming and making sand castles.

The sand dunes begin where the Humber flows into the North Sea and stretch most of the way southwards to Gibraltar Point. Except during high spring tides, the bases of these remain dry and are therefore excellent for picnics and for small children wishing to play in sand. In September the keen birdwatcher can see many migrant species feeding along the shoreline. A good place is at **Rimac**, near Saltfleet, a National Nature Reserve (TF 465923: near the junction of the A1031 and the B1200 from Louth). The other place for ornithologists is at **Gibraltar Point** (see page 62). Since the shore slopes so gently the tides come in very fast, and the unwary visitor can be cut off by deep gullies that fill rapidly once the tide turns.

One of the earliest inns that served visitors to the coast is the New Inn at **Saltfleet** (TF 454938), which was being frequented by coastal visitors as long ago as 1673. Other long-established seaside hotels include the Book-in-Hand at Mablethorpe (partially destroyed by fire in 1981 and now a shopping precinct) and the Vine at **Skegness** (where Tennyson stayed in the days when it was known as Enderby's Hotel). Near Boston on the **Freiston Shore** (TF 397423) stands Plummer's Hotel, built in the mid eighteenth century. Twentieth-century reclamation has left this high and dry, several fields from the

shores of the Wash. Nearby is the shell of its great rival the Marine Hotel.

For those who wish merely to drive up to the shore and sit in their cars enjoying seascapes, there are a number of pull-ins maintained for this purpose. Perhaps the most extensive and most panoramic is that at **Huttoft Bank**. This is at TF 542787, reached by turning seawards down a lane just to the north of Huttoft village on the A52 between Mablethorpe and Skegness. At very low tides part of a submerged prehistoric forest can be examined along the shore.

Two large holiday villages are **Chapel St Leonards** and Ingoldmells. The former was originally called Mumby Chapel (where a chapel of ease dedicated to St Leonard was built). Nowadays it is a favourite place for retired people to buy bungalows, but it also has chalets for hire, as well as holiday camps. **Ingoldmells** has caravan sites and a new amusement and shopping complex at the junction of Anchor Lane and Sea Lane. Just to the east of this is Ingoldmells Point, which is the most easterly part of the Lincolnshire shoreline.

For those seeking motor sports during their coastal vacations there is stock-car racing at the Skegness Stadium, situated just outside the village of Orby, reached by taking the lane that passes Ingoldmells church. There is also speedway motorcycle racing at the Boston Stadium. Cadwell Park, on the A153 to the south-west of Louth, has motorcycle racing (with the occasional car meeting) most Saturdays, Sundays and bank holiday Mondays.

The North Sea takes a long time to warm up each summer, especially if it has been a cold spring. There is a swimming pool at the Cleethorpes Leisure Centre, situated about half a mile (800 metres) south-east of the pier. If you are coming for the day it is advisable to listen to the local weather forecast before you

*This modern
statue of Havelock
the Dane in the
prow of his
longboat stands in
the grounds of
Havelock School,
Cleethorpes.*

start; if fog is promised for the coast, temperatures may be as much as 10 degrees Celsius lower than those inland.

Among other features along the Lincolnshire coast is the Viking gas terminal at Theddlethorpe. There are golf courses at Thrunscoe (Cleethorpes), Sandilands (Sutton-on-Sea), North Shore and Seacroft (Skegness).

When travelling to and from the coast allow plenty of time, especially during harvest, when tractors and combine harvesters can cause long tailbacks of traffic. In addition the A1031 (Cleethorpes to Mablethorpe) and A52 (Mablethorpe to Skegness) roads have innumerable bends that inhibit a fast journey, especially when there are caravans being towed along them.

12
Famous people

Sir Joseph Banks (1744-1820)

Born in London on 13th February 1744, Banks was educated at Eton and Oxford. In 1766, having been elected a Fellow of the Royal Society, he sailed to collect botanical specimens in Iceland and Newfoundland. In August 1768 he sailed with James Cook in the *Endeavour* to observe the transit of Venus from Tahiti and to gather more botanical specimens. He returned to England in 1771, having also visited Australia (where Botany Bay was named in his honour), New Zealand and New Guinea. He was elected President of the Royal Society and inherited the Revesby Abbey estate, between Horncastle and Spilsby and on the southern slopes of the Wolds. He also bought a town house in Horncastle (still to be seen on the corner of the Market Place) and commissioned a survey for a canal linking that town with the river Witham. He also commissioned the artist Nattes to sketch many venerable buildings then standing in the county. He died in July 1820.

George Bass (1771-1812)

This naval explorer was born at Aswarby, near Sleaford, in 1771, the son of a local farmer. After his parents died, he moved to Boston, where he was apprenticed to a surgeon. Upon qualifying, he took up a post in HMS *Reliance*, sailing for Sydney in 1795. He combined his medical duties with exploring the coast of New South Wales, and two years later circumnavigated Tasmania on a sloop captained by fellow Lincolnshireman Matthew Flinders. As a consequence the strait between this island and the Australian mainland was named in his honour.

William Cecil, first Baron Burghley (1520-98)

William Cecil was born in Bourne in 1520. After being educated at Cambridge and Gray's Inn, he was appointed Keeper of the Writs in the Court of Common Pleas by Henry VIII. In the next reign he became Master of Requests and then, in 1548, Secretary to Lord Protector Somerset. This led to his imprisonment by the succeeding Lord Protector Northumberland. However, he was soon reprieved and appointed Secretary of State. Although out of office during the reign of Mary I, he served the rest of his life as Chief Secretary to Elizabeth I, becoming Baron Burghley in 1571, by which time he was engaged on rebuilding Burghley House, near Stamford. He died on 4th August 1598 and is buried in the church of St Martin's Without in Stamford; his tomb is surmounted by an effigy of him holding his wand of office.

William Byrd (1543-1623)

Born somewhere in Lincolnshire, he became Senior Chorister at St Paul's Cathedral, being appointed organist at Lincoln Cathedral, a post he held from 1563 until 1572. Byrd co-operated with Thomas Tallis, John Bull and Orlando Gibbons in writing both secular and sacred music. He died on 4th July 1623.

Matthew Flinders (1774-1814)

Born at Donington to a family of surgeons, he decided to join the Royal Navy in 1790, after reading *Robinson Crusoe*. He sailed under Captain Bligh in HMS *Providence*. He helped George Bass survey the south-eastern coasts of Australia from 1795 until 1800. Upon the recommendation of Sir Joseph Banks he was placed in command of HMS *Investigator* on behalf of the East India Company, to survey the coast of New Holland, naming several features after places in his native county, e.g. Cape Donington, Boston Island and Spilsby Cove. In 1809 he was arrested in Mauritius by the French as a spy and was held for six months. When he returned to England he wrote up his voyages,

The isolated parish church at Sempringham, where St Gilbert founded his community of nuns.

dying on 19th July 1814. A model of his ship forms the weathervane on Partney church, where he was wed.

Sir John Franklin (1786-1847)

Born in Spilsby, he was the cousin of Matthew Flinders. Although intended for a career in the church, he went to sea as a merchant seaman before joining the Royal Navy in time to serve on HMS *Polyphemus* at the battle of Copenhagen (1801) and was on board HMS *Bellerophon* at the battle of Trafalgar four years later. His first expedition to America was in 1814, and during this he was slightly wounded at the battle of New Orleans. Four years later he took command of the brig HMS *Trent* in Captain Buchan's Arctic expedition, the first of a whole series of voyages of exploration in that area, which led to the award of its Gold Medal by the Geographical Society in 1827 and a knighthood in 1828. From 1836 until 1842 Franklin was Lieutenant Governor of Van Dieman's Land (Tasmania). His final Arctic voyage began in HMS *Erebus* in 1845 but, having been trapped by the ice in Victoria Strait, he died on 11th June 1847, along with his crew. His body was not discovered until 1859. The Franklin Mountains and Franklin Bay in northern Canada are named in his honour. There is a statue of him in Spilsby Market Place, erected in 1861.

St Gilbert of Sempringham (c.1083-1189)

The founder of the only English monastic order was born at Sempringham, near Sleaford. After becoming that village's priest in 1123, he drew up a rule for a group of young women living next to his church. Pope Eugenius III encouraged him to head a new monastic order obeying both the Rule of St Augustine (canons) and that of St Benedict (nuns). Henry II briefly imprisoned him, falsely accusing him of supporting Archbishop Thomas à Becket. Blind in old age, he died in 1189, supposedly aged 106, and was canonised in 1202, being given 16th February as his feast day. He founded in all twenty-six double houses of canons and nuns, ten of them in Lincolnshire.

Jean Ingelow (1820-97)

Born the daughter of a Boston banker, she had to move with her parents to Ipswich when her father's business collapsed. She became editor of the *Youth Magazine* and was soon well-known for her poetry. Her book entitled simply *Poems* brought her into contact with Tennyson, John Ruskin and Christina Rossetti. She also wrote novels, along with children's stories such as *Mopsa the Fairy* (1869), but she is best rembered for her poem *High Tide on the Coast of Lincolnshire, 1571* (based on what she had learnt in Boston about a similar incursion of the sea in 1810). Like Christina Rossetti, she was turned down by Queen Victoria as a possible successor to Tennyson as Poet Laureate. She died on 20th July 1897.

Herbert Ingram (1811-60)

Born in Boston, he was educated at the Free School in that town, before being apprenticed as a printer. Later he moved to London to continue this trade in 1832. After he gained more experience he started to print on his own and became a bookseller in Nottingham. However, the profits he made from a sideline, selling Thomas Parr's Vegetable Pills, enabled him to launch the *Illustrated London News* on 14th May 1842. By 1852 circulation had reached 250,000 with the edition covering the funeral of the Duke of Wellington. In 1856 he was elected MP for Boston. He was drowned in Lake Michigan on 8th September 1860 when the *Lady Elgin* sank following a collision. In Boston he is chiefly remembered for launching the company that provided the port with an adequate water supply in 1849, this being portrayed in his statue's plinth outside Boston Stump.

Sir Isaac Newton (1642-1727)

Several places in the Grantham area connected with Isaac Newton, the scientist, mathematician, philosopher and Master of the Mint, can be visited. He was born on Christmas Day 1642 at **Woolsthorpe Manor**, Woolsthorpe-by-Colsterworth. Built *c.*1620 of local limestone, the house is now in the care of the National Trust and is open to the public at certain times. Here the visitor can see not only a collection of Newton relics, but also some of his early geometrical scratchings on the plasterwork. It was to Woolsthorpe that the great scholar retreated during the plague of 1665-6 and there he discovered differential calculus, the composition of white light and the law of gravitation.

Across the narrow valley of the Witham is the parish church of St John the Baptist at **Colsterworth**, where the Newtons would have worshipped (apart from the winter months when they may well have gone to the small chapel of ease at Woolsthorpe, now a private cottage). At Colsterworth the young Newton carved a sundial on the church wall.

He is said to have begun his education at dame schools in the nearby churches of **Stoke Rochford** (in those days normally called South Stoke) and **Skillington**. In the grounds of Stoke Rochford Hall (now a training college for officials of the National Union of Teachers) stands an obelisk erected in the

Sir Isaac Newton's statue in the centre of Grantham.

nineteenth century in his memory. He continued his education at King's School in Grantham in a building that dates from 1497 on the corner of Castlegate, opposite the north side of St Wulfram's church. In 1859 a statue of Newton was unveiled on St Peter's Hill in the centre of the town, opposite the museum, which contains a display of various items connected with his life.

Captain John Smith (1580-1631)

Born at Willoughby, south of Alford, in January 1580, John Smith spent his schooldays at the King Edward VI Grammar School in **Louth**, where a plaque in the school hall and a mural celebrate this, although none of the original buildings remains. After two spells as a mercenary soldier in Europe, he left England for Virginia with 104 emigrants, arriving at Chesapeake Bay on 26th April 1607. As governor of the colony he had many problems, not least of which were the local Red Indians. He was rescued from certain death by a chieftain's daughter, Pocahontas, whom he subsequently brought back to England. Between his final return to England in 1617 and his death in June 1631 he published several books and maps on the New World.

At **Willoughby** there is a portrait of Smith painted on the exterior wall of the Willoughby Arms. In the nearby parish church of St Helen there is a fine memorial window to him, a gift from admirers in the United States. When he was at home Smith liked to study in the local woods, and the village is still surrounded by these. His reputed home is to be found in the lane that passes the church; the roof of this Tudor farmhouse has been lowered in modern times.

William Stukeley (1687-1765)

Born in Barrington Gate, Holbeach, in 1687, William Stukeley became not only a doctor of medicine but also an Anglican priest. However, he is best-known for his antiquarian and archaeological research, which unfortunately became dominated in his later years by an obsession with druids. Nevertheless, he saved many of the stones from the great circle at Avebury (Wiltshire) from certain destruction and he also formulated theories about Stonehenge. His chronicle of his journeys, entitled *Itinerarium Curiosum* (published in 1724), is still a useful source book for local historians.

Stukeley was vicar of All Saints, **Stamford**, from 1729 until 1747, and this church is substantially the same as when he was its incumbent. At the back of All Saints Place is Barn Hill, where the present Stukeley House stands on the site of the one he occupied. It dates from 1741. Off the B1176 near Grantham is the church of St Mary Magdalen, **Old Somerby**, which Stukeley held in plurality with All Saints, Stamford. Although it was partially restored in the nineteenth century, the Norman and Early English work is the same as it was in his time.

Alfred, Lord Tennyson (1809-92)

Born on 6th August 1809 at the Rectory at **Somersby**, near Spilsby, Alfred Tennyson was educated for a few years at the King Edward VI Grammar School in **Louth**. He stayed with a relative at Harvey's Court, a narrow alleyway leading off the north side of Westgate, near the Wheatsheaf Inn. A plaque marks the house, near the banks of the river Lud. He was unhappy at the school and eventually persuaded his father, the Reverend Dr George Tennyson, to act as his tutor at Somersby. His father's grave can be easily found in the churchyard of St Margaret's, almost opposite the Rectory (which is not open to the public). In 1827 Alfred and his elder brother, Charles, had their *Poems by Two Brothers* published by J. and J. Jackson in Louth Market Place. A plaque on the premises (now Oxfam) commemorates this event.

Tennyson's poem 'The Brook' is based loosely on the stream that passes through Somersby, before becoming first the river Lymm (best seen near Ashby-by-Partney on the A1115) and then the Steeping River (as at Wainfleet on the A52).

There are some small mementoes and a bust of the Poet Laureate in Somersby church. His statue (complete with wolfhound) stands outside the chapter house at **Lincoln Cathedral**; it was designed by George Frederick Watts in 1905. There is a collection of items

The bust of Alfred, Lord Tennyson, in Somersby church and, right, the Rectory, in which he was born.

connected with Tennyson in the **Usher Gallery**, Lincoln. **Gunby Hall** also has associations with the poet.

Between 1828 and 1843 Tennyson stayed on occasions as the guest of a Mrs Wiliman at Marine Villa, **Mablethorpe**. This property still stands, having been reroofed in 1983 and whitewashed. It is now called Tennyson's Cottage and is about four minutes' walk northwards along the road that leads from the pullover at the sea end of High Street towards North End. It stands back from the road between Cornhill Cottage and Beckside Lodge but it is not open to the public. In later years the poet also stayed at what was then called Enderby's Hotel at **Seacroft**, Skegness. Nowadays it is called The Vine.

Reverend John Benjamin Wesley (1703-91)

The fifteenth child of the Reverend Samuel Wesley, rector of Epworth, and his wife Susanna, John was rescued from the famous rectory fire caused by local arsonists in 1709.

After being educated at the rectory by his mother, he was sent to Charterhouse School, and thence to Oxford University, where he became a lecturer in Greek. In 1727 he returned to Epworth to act as his father's curate, but when his parents died he emigrated to Georgia, where he was joined by his younger brother Charles. After a disastrous time amongst the colonists, he returned to England in 1738, when he felt called to evangelise Britain and, under the influence of George Whitfield, he took up field preaching. He often revisited his native county, making particular friends with farmer Robinson of Langham Row (near Chapel St Leonards) and squire Robert Carr Brackenbury of Raithby-by-Spilsby. He wrote works as varied as *Notes on the New Testament* and *Primitive Physic* (1747), as well as translating hymns, especially from German. He died at the City Road Chapel, London, on 2nd March 1791, after travelling some 250,000 miles (400,000 km) in all and founding the Methodist movement.

John Whitgift (c.1530-1604)

The nephew of the last Abbot of Wellow (Grimsby), Whitgift was born in that port, but educated at St Anthony's School in London and at Cambridge University, where he held several posts, including those of Regius Professor of Divinity, Master of Trinity College and eventually Vice-Chancellor. At the same time he was Bishop of Ely and for a while Dean of Lincoln and Rector of Laceby (near Grimsby). However, he is chiefly renowned as Elizabeth I's third and final Archbishop of Canterbury, to which position he was elected in 1583. He was a strict Calvinist but at the same time defended the Church of England stoutly in its Thirty-nine Articles. He crowned James I in 1603 and attended the Hampton Court Conference, which resulted in the Authorised Version of the Bible (the King James Bible). He died on 29th February 1604.

The medieval cross in Epworth's Market Place, where John Wesley preached.

13
The shire year

Kirton-in-Lindsey Bells

As at some other places at New Year, the bells of St Andrew's church are rung, starting at about 11.30 p.m. on New Year's Eve. They are rung half-muffled for twenty minutes, then the muffles are removed ready for midnight. The tenor bell strikes twelve, and immediately afterwards all eight bells peal in the New Year.

Haxey Hood Game

According to legend it was on Twelfth Night that the wife of Sir John de Mowbray was riding on horseback across the fields near Haxey on the Isle of Axholme, when a sudden gust of wind blew away her large black silk hood. Thirteen labourers in a nearby field gave chase to rescue it, vying with one another to return it to its graceful owner. She was so grateful that she donated a piece of land on Westwood Hill, just outside the village, for an annual enactment of the gallant recovery of her hood. Whether this is true or not, the Haxey Hood Game still takes place on 6th January each year. A 'Fool' dressed in patched trousers and red jumper begins the proceedings, swinging a bladder (now a stuffed sock) attached to a stick. He mounts a stone outside Haxey parish church and calls out: 'Hoose agin hoose, toon agin toon, If tha meet a man, knock him doon, But doan't hu't 'im.' Damp straw is then set alight under him; this is known as 'smoking the Fool'.

The two 'toons' in this challenge are Haxey and the neighbouring hamlet of West-woodside. Teams of young men from each village then form a massive scrum, with up to fifty on each side, and attempt to push their opponents, and the Hood, to the pub of their choice. This (the 'Sway') may last for several hours before the Hood is delivered to one of the pubs, where it remains for the ensuing year. The Hood no longer resembles a lady's head covering but is a cylinder of tough leather. Other characters taking part are the Lord of the Hood, who carries a willow wand or staff of office, the Chief Boggan and ten ordinary Boggans, all of whom wear red jumpers.

Plough Sunday

Since 1943 this has replaced the traditional Plough Monday (the first after Twelfth Night) with its 'jags'. A plough is brought into the church 'to offer the work of the countryside to the service of God', and the implement is blessed, along with the agricultural workers of that parish.

North Somercotes Pancake Races

In imitation of the long-established Olney event on Shrove Tuesday, participants run the length of this linear village on the Lindsey coastline tossing their pancakes. There are two classes: for adults and for children.

Red Hill Good Friday Service

Red Hill, Goulceby (OS 122: TF 264806), situated high in the Wolds to the south-west of Louth, consists of an outcrop of rare red chalk, which lies above a stratum of khaki-coloured carstone. Belemnites and other fossils abound in it, and an old chalk pit here is surrounded by one of the last small fragments of grassland, now in the safe keeping of the Lincolnshire Trust for Nature Conservation.

Each Good Friday morning a procession forms at the foot of the hill, led by the incumbent of the tiny church of Asterby and three parishioners carrying crosses, and followed by several hundred local people and visitors. They slowly climb the steep lane to the chalk pit. Dramatically silhouetted against the skyline, the three crosses are erected on the lip of the pit, and then a short service follows in the pit, the singing being accompanied by the Horncastle Silver Band.

Spalding Tulip Parade

A nationally famous event held in Lincolnshire each year is the procession of decorated floats through the streets of Spalding usually on the first Saturday afternoon in May. Unless visitors plan to travel on one of the hundreds of coaches or two dozen trains bringing spectators for this colourful event, they should aim to reach the town well before midday, since they may have a long distance to walk through dense crowds from their car park to an advantageous position along the route. Perhaps the least crowded place to watch the spectacle is in the suburb of Fulney (along the A151 Holbeach road) in Queen's Road.

The first parade was held in 1959 and since then the size and complexity of the floats have grown enormously. Each year a theme is chosen, and a commercial artist draws up the designs for each float. Then, as early as November, a local blacksmith begins to construct the steel framework, using 12 miles (20 km) of metal strip each year. A month later the immense task of covering the frames with rye straw matting is started, using six hundred imported mats, each 10 by 6 feet (3 by 2 metres), for each parade. Finally, in the last forty-eight hours before the parade, millions of tulip heads are carefully attached to the matting. In addition there are static displays made up of tulip heads, sponsored by local organisations, at places throughout the town (for example, by the tower of the parish church of St Mary and St Nicholas).

'Miss Tulipland' and her deputy are selected from local girls and ride high on the leading floats, accompanied by their ladies-in-waiting.

Each float is preceded by a band, military or otherwise, and many of the bands come from distant parts of Britain.

Both in Spalding and in the surrounding villages, floral displays are presented in parish and nonconformist churches, and often teas are served for visitors. In some areas of the Fens near Spalding during this weekend one-way systems operate along the narrow lanes that skirt the vast tulip fields, and special routes for sightseers are well signposted and worth following.

Lincoln Water Festival

Each year since 1973 the first weekend in June has been celebrated on Brayford Pool in the centre of Lincoln by a wide-ranging Water Festival. This is a regatta with a difference, which raises a great deal of money for charities. There are various rowing and sailing races, serious and otherwise, whilst the City Carnival procession parades round the Pool on land after proceeding through the streets in the centre of Lincoln. A small fair and a larger number of exhibition stands (not all of them directly connected with water) line the crowded north bank of Brayford. In side streets such as Lucy Tower Street there are other attractions. Crowds of up to one hundred thousand attend when the weather is fine. There are no charges for admission, but programmes are on sale in aid of charities.

Lincolnshire Show

Held on a Wednesday and Thursday in late June each year, since 1959 the Lincolnshire Show has taken place on the permanent site acquired by the Lincolnshire Agricultural Society beside the A15 to the north of Lincoln. It was first held in 1869. One of the rings stands at the junction of Ermine Street, a Roman road, and the equally old Tillbridge Lane, and is appropriately called the Roman Ring.

Although the Lincolnshire Curly Coat pig has become extinct, the Lincolnshire Show gives an opportunity to see another distinctive local breed, the Lincoln Red cattle. A third Lincolnshire breed is the Longwool sheep, and the breed's society has its offices at the showground. The show's emphasis is on agricultural machinery, and this part of it is the second largest of its kind in Britain.

The showjumping attracts leading competitors. There are also spectacular displays staged by members of the armed forces and amusing contests between the many Young Farmers' Clubs in the county. Attendances may exceed eighty thousand in good weather.

The Sandtoft Gathering

On the last Sunday in July each year thousands of transport enthusiasts converge on the disused airfield at Sandtoft on the Isle of

Axholme (OS 112: SE 750081). It can be reached either from the A18 or else by leaving the M180 at junction 2, travelling south along the A161 to Belton and then turning right and continuing for about 3 miles (5 km). There is a procession of old buses and coaches, accompanied by vintage cars and commercial vehicles, from Doncaster Racecourse to Sandtoft in the morning (arriving about noon). As well as a flea market, there is a chance to ride on several preserved and restored trolleybuses (for further details of the museum here see page 99).

Alford Festival

The Alford Festival grew out of a craft market established in this small town at the foot of the Wolds in 1974 and followed by a craft weekend the following summer. Now up to thirty thousand people attend the three-day festival, held over the Late Summer Bank Holiday weekend at the end of August. As well as a considerable variety of craftwork on display and for sale, an extensive art exhibition is staged in Alford Methodist Church, and there are floral displays there and in St Wilfrid's parish church, mass displays of morris dancing by both male and female troupes, and 'fringe' theatre in a marquee situated at the rear of the Old Manor House in West Street.

Cadwell Park Vintage Racing Cars Meeting

Although normally associated with motorcycle races, Cadwell Park (on the A153 to the south-west of Louth) stages a very popular meeting on the Sunday afternoon of the Late Summer Bank Holiday in which the Bugattis and ERAs of the inter-war years compete against each other again on this picturesque circuit high up on the Wolds. There are even earlier racing cars in action on occasions.

Burghley Horse Trials

In 1960 the sixth Marquis of Exeter agreed to allow the British Horse Society to move its Autumn Trials from Harewood House in West Yorkshire to Burghley Park on the outskirts of Stamford, where they now take place at the end of the first or second week in September. The World Three Day Event Championships were held here in 1966 and 1974. The trials attract large crowds, so the visitor needs to arrive on the B1443 road in good time for the start of the day's events. On the Friday the dressage competition is held in the main arena. The most popular day is the Saturday, when the competitors have to cover two phases of roads and tracks on the Burghley estate, in between which they have to jump a steeplechase course. Finally they have to cover the gruelling cross-country course with its twenty-seven assorted obstacles, of which the most notorious is the Upper Trout Hatchery (where even royal riders have received a ducking). On the Sunday afternoon the competitors take part in the showjumping contest.

Elsewhere in the park, pony clubs from all over Lincolnshire, East Anglia and the East Midlands compete in their own contests. There are many trade stands and two large marquees filled with a great variety of rural crafts.

Eastern International Air Fair

This is held at Humberside Airport on the A18 on the first Sunday in August. As well as a flying display by modern and vintage aircraft, there are parachute falls and the Royal Aero Club City Livery Trophy Race.

Other events

In addition to the events detailed above there are many village shows, two of the principal ones being staged at **Heckington** (on the A17 between Sleaford and Boston) and at **Winterton** (on the A1077). There are a number of village 'feasts' still held, such as that at **Osbournby** (on the A15 between Bourne and Sleaford) on the second Saturday in July, when a Lincolnshire delicacy, stuffed chine, is served. There are also bank holiday race meetings at **Market Rasen**.

14
Food and folklore

Grantham gingerbread

There are various recipes for Grantham gingerbread, differing in the proportions of sugar and butter or margarine used. In some cases an egg is added, but they all agree that the mixture should be rolled into balls described in size variously as walnuts, marbles or small golf balls! They all state that the final product should appear light in colour and not dark brown as is usually associated with ginger foods. *McDougall's Cookery Book* gives the ingredients as $1/4$ pound (113 grams) self raising flour, $1/4$ pound castor sugar, 1 pound butter or margarine, 2 level teaspoons ground ginger and 1 beaten egg. Cream the fat and sugar together, then sieve the flour and ground ginger. Add the egg to the fat and sugar mix, and work in the flour and ginger until it forms a stiff dough. Roll into balls, and place on a greased tin in an oven for 45 minutes at regulo mark 1 (143°C).

Haslet

Often pronounced 'ays-zlet', haslet is the traditional cold meat loaf of Lincolnshire. Its basic ingredient is blooded pieces of pork that are not good enough to be made into pies or sausages. These are minced finely. To this are added 1 pound (454 grams) of pig's liver, 1 cup of finely crumbled bread, 1 ounce (28 grams) of green sage, salt and pepper. Once they have been mixed well together they are wrapped in a pig's apron (the lining of a pig's stomach) and baked in a moderate oven for two hours. It is then left in a tin until cold before being served.

Samphire

The plant samphire (pronounced 'samfer'), or glasswort, grows on the saltmarshes of the Lincolnshire coast. Traditionally samphire harvesting day is August Bank Holiday Mon-

day, but it can be gathered as early as June. At the latter time the shoots should be pinched off above the roots. In July and August the whole plant can be pulled up. It should be boiled upside down in a saucepan of water, drained and served with melted butter and stuffed chine. It can also be pickled in vinegar and served as a salad.

Lincolnshire folklore

There is a whole corpus of weather lore still remembered, especially in the more rural areas of the county. The following are some examples of this:

24th February
St Matthew breaks the ice; if he finds none he will make it.

2nd March (St Chad's Day)
Sow your beans.
Four seeds in each hole.
One for pigeon, one for crow,
One to wither and one to grow.

1st April
If it thunders on All Fools Day, it brings good crops of corn and hay.

25th April
When St George growls in the sky, wind and storm are drawing nigh.

18th October (St Luke's Day)
Thunder in the morning signifies wind,
Thunder at noon signifies rain,
Thunder in the evening signifies storm.

Autumn generally
Much fog in autumn, much snow in winter.
If foxes bark much in October, a heavy fall of snow may be expected.

15
Tours for motorists

Gainsborough, Morton, along the right bank of the Trent via Walkerith, East Stockwith, Wildsworth and East Ferry to Susworth, then to Scotter, Scotton, Kirton-in-Lindsey, Grayingham, Blyborough, Willoughton, Hemswell, across A631 to Springthorpe, Heapham, Upton, Kexby, Willingham-by-Stow, Stow St Mary, Marton, along A156 to Torksey, back through Marton to Knaith, Lea and Gainsborough. (This route can be achieved in two sections by dividing it between Hemswell and Springthorpe, by driving along the A631.)

Grantham, Londonthorpe, Welby, Oasby, Ropsley, Sapperton, Pickworth, Walcot, Folkingham, Billingborough, Sempringham, Pointon, Dowsby, Rippingale, Dunsby, Hacconby, Morton, Bourne, along A151 to Edenham and Grimsthorpe Castle, Swinstead, Corby Glen, Burton Coggles (off B1176), Bassingthorpe, Great Ponton, Grantham.

Grimsby via A1036 through Little Coates, Great Coates and Healing to Stallingborough, then to Keelby, via B1211 through Brocklesby and Ulceby to Wootton, via A1077 to Thornton Curtis, then Thornton Abbey, Goxhill, Barrow-upon-Humber, via A1077 to Barton-upon-Humber and South Ferriby, via B1204 through Horkstow, Saxby All Saints, Bonby, Worlaby and Elsham to Wrawby, via A18 into Brigg, then via A1084 through Bigby, Searby, Owmby, Grasby and Clixby to Caistor, returning via A46 through Cabourne, Swallow, Irby-on-Humber and Laceby to Grimsby. (This route can be achieved in two sections by using the A18.)

Lincoln, via B1190 through Washingborough to Bardney, retrace route as far as junction with B1202 for Potterhanworth and Nocton, via B1188 to Metheringham, Blankney, and Scopwick, thence via B1191 through Ashby-de-la-Launde, cross over A15 for Temple Bruer and Welbourn, cross A607 for Brant Broughton, Stragglethorpe (across the A17), Brandon, Stubton, Fenton, Beckingham (on A17), Stapleford, Norton Disney, Thurlby-by-Lincoln, Haddington, South Hykeham, North Hykeham, Lincoln. (The route can be achieved in two sections by dividing it along the A607 between Lincoln and Welbourn.)

Louth, via B1200, turning off to Little Cawthorpe, Muckton, Belleau, South Thoresby, Haugh, Rigsby, Well (across the A1104), via B1196 through Willoughby-in-the-Marsh and Welton-le-Marsh to Gunby, via A158 through Candlesby and Scremby to Partney, on along the A158 to Sausthorpe and Hagworthingham, turn right for Stockwith Mill, Harrington, Bag Enderby, Somersby, Tetford, Ruckland, Haugham, and back to Louth along Al6.

Spalding, via A1073 to Cowbit, Brotherhouse and Crowland, then back to junction with B1166, along this road to Postland, Shepeau Stow and Holbeach Drove, via B1168 through Holbeach St John to Saturday Bridge crossroads, right along B1165 to Sutton St James, bearing left for Tydd St Mary, along A1101 to Long Sutton, cross A17 for Lutton and return to A17 for Gedney and Fleet Hargate, via A151 through Holbeach, Whaplode, Moulton and Weston to Spalding.

16
Further reading

Beckwith, Ian. *The Book of Gainsborough*. Barracuda, 1988.
Beckwith, Ian. *The Book of Lincoln*. Barracuda, 1990.
Hill, Sir Francis. *Medieval Lincoln*. Cambridge University Press, 1965.
Hill, Sir Francis. *Georgian Lincoln*. Cambridge University Press, 1966.
Hill, Sir Francis. *Victorian Lincoln*. Cambridge University Press, 1974.
Hill, Sir Francis. *Tudor and Stuart Lincoln*. Cambridge University Press, 1991.
Honeybone, Michael. *The Book of Grantham*. Barracuda, 1980.
Kaye, David. *The Book of Grimsby*. Barracuda, 1981.
Kaye, David, and Scorer, Sam. *Fowler of Louth*. Louth Antiquarian and Literary Society, 1992.
Kime, Winston. *The Book of Skegness*. Barracuda, 1986.
Leary, William. *Lincolnshire Methodism*. Barracuda, 1988.
May, Jeffery. *Prehistoric Lincolnshire*. History of Lincolnshire Committee, 1976.
Mills, Dennis, *et al. Twentieth Century Lincolnshire*. History of Lincolnshire Committee, 1989.
Pevsner, Sir Nikolaus, *et al. The Buildings of England: Lincolnshire*. Penguin, 1989.
Robinson, David N. *The Book of the Lincolnshire Seaside*. Barracuda, 1981.
Robinson, David N. *The Book of Horncastle and Woodhall Spa*. Barracuda, 1983.
Robinson, David N. *The Book of Louth*. Barracuda, 1979.
Rogers, Alan. *The Book of Stamford*. Barracuda, 1983.
Rogers, Alan. *A History of Lincolnshire*. Phillimore, 1985.
Tyszka, Dinah, *et al. Land, People and Landscapes*. Lincolnshire County Council, 1991.
Whitwell, Ben. *Roman Lincolnshire*. History of Lincolnshire Committee, 1992.
Wright, Neil R. *Lincolnshire Towns and Industry, 1700-1914*. History of Lincolnshire Committee, 1982.
Wright, Neil R. *The Book of Boston*. Barracuda, 1986.
Young, Arthur. *General View of the Agriculture of the County of Lincolnshire, 1813*. David & Charles reprint, 1970.

17
Tourist information centres

Boston: Blackfriars Arts Centre, Spain Lane, Boston PE21 6HP. Telephone: 01205 356656.
Brigg: The Buttercross, Market Place, Brigg DN20 8ER. Telephone: 01652 657053.
Cleethorpes: 42/43 Alexandra Road, Cleethorpes DN35 8LE. Telephone: 01472 200220.
Gainsborough: The Guildhall, Gainsborough DN21 2DH. Telephone: 01427 615411.
Grantham: St Peter's Hill, Grantham NG31 6PZ. Telephone: 01476 66444.
Grimsby: Heritage Centre, Alexandra Dock, Grimsby DN31 1UF. Telephone: 01472 342422.
Lincoln: 9 Castle Hill, Lincoln LN1 3AA. Telephone: 01522 529828.
Lincoln (East Midlands Tourist Board): Exchequergate, Lincoln LN2 1PZ. Telephone: 01522 531521.
Louth: New Market Hall, Louth LN11 9PY. Telephone: 01507 526636.
Mablethorpe: The Dunes, Central Promenade, Mablethorpe LN12 1RG. Telephone: 01507 472496.
Scunthorpe: Civic Centre, Ashby Road, Scunthorpe DN16 1AB. Telephone: 01724 280444.
Skegness: Embassy Centre, Grand Parade, Skegness PE25 2UG. Telephone: 01754 764821.
Sleaford: The Mill, Money's Yard, Carre Street, Sleaford NG34 7TW. Telephone: 01529 488490.
Spalding: Ayscoughfee Hall, Churchgate, Spalding PE11 2RA. Telephone: 01775 725468.
Stamford: Stamford Arts Centre, St Mary's Street, Stamford PE9 2DR. Telephone: 01786 455611.

The 1821 Town Hall in the Market Place, Bourne.

Index

Page numbers in italic type refer to illustrations.